Pastor Wendy

RALPH WALDO EMERSON

MODERN SPIRITUAL MASTERS SERIES

RALPH WALDO EMERSON

Essential Spiritual Writings

Selected with an Introduction by
JON M. SWEENEY

ORBIS BOOKS
Maryknoll, New York 10545

ORBIS BOOKS
Maryknoll, New York 10545

Fathers and Brothers
MARYKNOLL

Founded in 1970, Orbis Books endeavors to publish works that enlighten the mind, nourish the spirit, and challenge the conscience. The publishing arm of the Maryknoll Fathers and Brothers, Orbis seeks to explore the global dimensions of the Christian faith and mission, to invite dialogue with diverse cultures and religious traditions, and to serve the cause of reconciliation and peace. The books published reflect the views of their authors and do not represent the official position of the Maryknoll Society. To learn more about Maryknoll and Orbis Books, please visit our website at www.maryknollsociety.org.

Library of Congress Cataloging-in-Publication Data

Emerson, Ralph Waldo, 1803-1882.
[Works. Selections. 2016]
Essential writings / Ralph Waldo Emerson ; selected with an introduction by Jon M. Sweeney.
    pages cm. -- (Modern spiritual masters series)
  Includes bibliographical references.
  ISBN 978-1-62698-177-5 (pbk.)
  I. Sweeney, Jon M., 1967- II. Title.
PS1603.S93 2016
814'.3—dc23
2015030109

To Gary Masquelier, who first taught me,
"In the woods, we return to reason and faith."

Contents

5. **"WISE ANCIENT WOODS"**

Sources

Essays: First	*Essays: First Series* (1841)
Essays: Second	*Essays: Second Series* (1844)
Poems	*Poems* (1847)
Nature	*Nature, Addresses, and Lectures* (1849)
Men	*Representative Men* (1850)
Traits	*English Traits* (1856)
Atlantic Monthly	RWE's translations of Hafiz published in *Atlantic Monthly* (April 1958)
Conduct	*The Conduct of Life* (1860)
May-Day	*May-Day and Other Pieces* (1867)
Solitude	*Society and Solitude* (1870)
Sketches	*Lectures and Biographical Sketches*, Edward W. Emerson ed. (1883)
Early Poems	*Early Poems of Ralph Waldo Emerson* (1899)
Miscellanies	*The Works of Ralph Waldo Emerson* (1899)
Journals 1820–1842	*Selected Journals, 1820–1842*, ed. by Lawrence Rosenwald. New York: Library of America, 2010.
Journals 1841–1877	*Selected Journals, 1841–1877*, ed. by Lawrence Rosenwald. New York: Library of America, 2010.

SELECTED SECONDARY SOURCES

Ahlstrom, Sydney, and Jonathan S. Carey. *An American Reformation: A Documentary History of Unitarian Christianity*. Middletown, CT: Wesleyan University Press, 1985.

Buell, Lawrence (ed). *The American Transcendentalists: Essential Writings*. New York: Modern Library, 2006.

———. *Emerson*. Cambridge, MA: Harvard University Press, 2003.

LaRocca, David (ed). *Estimating Emerson: An Anthology of Criticism from Carlyle to Cavell*. New York: Bloomsbury, 2013.

Matthiessen, F. O. *American Renaissance: Art and Expression in the Age of Emerson and Whitman*. New York: Oxford University Press, 1968.

Richardson, Robert D., Jr. *Emerson: The Mind on Fire*. Berkeley: University of California Press, 1995.

von Frank, Albert J. (chief ed.). *The Complete Sermons of Ralph Waldo Emerson in Four Volumes*. Columbia: University of Missouri Press, 1989–92.

Chronology

1803   Ralph Waldo Emerson [RWE] born in Boston on May 25, son of Ruth Haskins and Rev. William Emerson.

1811   Rev. William Emerson, a Unitarian minister, dies at age forty-two.

1817–21   RWE attends Harvard College, graduating at age eighteen, "a surprisingly conventional young man" and a traditional, creedal, Christian.[1]

1822–28   Teaches school. Travels in the American South to restore his health; witnesses slavery firsthand. Spends three years studying at the new Harvard Divinity School.

1829   Ordained a Unitarian minister like his father. Becomes junior pastor of Second Church, Boston. Marries Ellen Tucker.

1831   Ellen dies of tuberculosis at age nineteen.

1832   Resigns his pastorate because he can no longer in good conscience administer the sacrament of Communion. In letter of resignation, September 11, RWE concludes, "I should be unfaithful to myself, if any change of circumstances could diminish my devotion to the cause of divine truth."[2] Sails for Europe on December 25.

1833   Visits Malta, Italy, France, Scotland, and England. Meets Carlyle, Coleridge, Mill, and Wordsworth. Sails back to America in September.

1834   His brilliant younger brother, Edward, dies of tuberculosis.

1835   Marries Lydia Jackson. Declines another pastorate but continues to preach and lecture often.

1836   Brother Charles dies, devastating RWE. First essay, *Nature*, is published by James Munroe and Company, less than one hundred pages—anonymously. Writes preface to Thomas Carlyle's *Sartor Resartus*, which is published in Boston at RWE's expense. Leads effort to meet regularly with Alcott, Brownson, Fuller, and others in Boston in what comes to be called The Transcendental Club.

1837   Delivers the now-famous "American Scholar" address to the Phi Beta Kappa Society in Cambridge. Meets Thoreau, who graduates from Harvard. Receives large sum from Ellen's estate, putting him on firm financial footing.

1839   Preaches his final sermon in church.

1841   Thoreau comes to live in RWE's home.

       Five years after *Nature* was published as a pamphlet, RWE reissues it with lectures delivered over the last five years, this time under his own name, as *Essays: First Series*.

1842   Son Waldo dies at age five from scarlet fever.

1844   *Essays: Second Series* is published. Purchases land on Walden Pond. With   RWE's   permission, Thoreau builds a hut there the following year. Twenty-six months into his stay, Thoreau's experiment in simple living is cut short by RWE's asking him to live in town, in RWE's home, while RWE journeys to England.

1847   *Poems* is published.

1849   *Nature; Addresses, and Lectures* is published.

1850   *Representative Men* is published. RWE's friend and colleague, Margaret Fuller, dies in a shipwreck.

1851–59   Lectures widely against slavery; defends and lionizes John Brown.

1855   Walt Whitman publishes *Leaves of Grass*, inspired by RWE's 1844 essay, "The Poet."

1856   *English Traits* is published.

1858   RWE's translations of Hafiz are published in the April issue of *Atlantic Monthly*.

1860   *The Conduct of Life* is published.

1862   Thoreau dies May 6; RWE speaks at his funeral, vowing that Americans will soon learn how great a man Thoreau was.

1865   Edits and publishes *Letters to Various Persons*, by Henry D. Thoreau.

1867   *May-Day and Other Pieces* is published.

1870   *Society and Solitude* is published.

1882   RWE dies of pneumonia on April 27.

1883   *Lectures and Biographical Sketches* (Edward W. Emerson, editor) is published.

1899   *Early Poems of Ralph Waldo Emerson* is published.

1909   *The Works of Ralph Waldo Emerson, Vol. 11 (Miscellanies)* is published.

Introduction

The Sage of Concord remains an enormous figure on the historical spectrum of American intellectual and cultural life, but it would be difficult to make the same claim for his writings in the early twenty-first century. Some men and women lived so large that their lives blur their writings.

This is what happened to Abraham Lincoln, the other larger-than-life public intellectual of the mid-nineteenth century. The sixteenth president of the United States suffered from an unjust neglect of his oeuvre. Until quite recently, although much discussed as one of his century's most pivotal historical figures, Lincoln was rarely read. It has only been over the last two decades that a wide readership has once again become acquainted with Lincoln's writings, and he's become more than a man on the world stage: a man of ideas.

Emerson's life wasn't as dramatic as Lincoln's, and telling the story of that life, of its place in the history of American religion and letters, has often become a way to avoid his actual writings.[3] The situation was actually reversed during Emerson's lifetime. For a half-century, beginning in the late 1830s, Americans hung on his words while taking little notice of what happened in his life. His writings are, in fact, the only reason why Emerson is, or ever intended to be, an important figure in history. This volume aims to address this irony and unjust neglect. A collection of his most important spiritual ideas and reflections, this collection of Emerson's words aims to actually demonstrate why he was Concord's sage.

* * *

After this Introduction, all of Emerson's writings in this volume are taken from his published, written work. No journal passages, personal letters, table talk, or sermon quotations are found in the body of the book, unless they also appeared in his published books and essays. There are three reasons for this. First, I wanted to offer a portrait of the mature Emerson. Delivering a sermon is a form of publishing one's sentiments and opinions, and Emerson filled several volumes worth of sermons from 1826 to 1839, but he also left behind the preaching of sermons in churches at about the same time that his thought developed into its most mature form. This book isn't meant to chart the growth of the mind of its subject; others make that Emerson easily available. See, in particular, the new *Portable Emerson*, edited by Jeffrey S. Cramer for Penguin Classics (2014). Instead, you will encounter here all of Emerson's essential, mature, religious, and spiritual thought.

Second, I have left out quotations from letters, diaries, and the like because I want to offer a portrait that would most faithfully match what was available to any resident of Concord, Boston, New England, America, and Europe during Emerson's lifetime, who was interested in what the leading light of Transcendentalism thought and said. Only here in the Introduction, and occasionally in the short introductions to the writings, will readers find references to Emerson's more private forms of communication, for purposes of setting up a theme or individual piece.

Third, unlike his friend Thoreau, Emerson published so much during his lifetime that one doesn't need to *fill in the gaps* with reference to private journals and letters.[4] There is plenty of material upon which an editor may draw.

HIS PLACE AND TIME

The Parker House Hotel stands in the oldest neighborhood of Boston, on School Street near Tremont. This grand dame of hospitality, built in 1855, only a year later became home to a monthly gathering called the Saturday Club. There, Ralph Waldo Emerson, Henry David Thoreau, Charles Peirce, Arthur Wendell Holmes, Henry Wadsworth Longfellow, and other intellectuals would drink and dine together, discussing issues of the day. They were akin to the early twentieth-century Bloomsbury Group in London's Russell Square or the Algonquin Roundtable in mid-town Manhattan—except that the Saturday Club was made up, not only of a nation's literati, but its leading thinkers.

The Parker House is rich with associations. The nineteenth century's greatest novelist, Charles Dickens, resided there for two years while composing *A Christmas Carol*. John Wilkes Booth stayed in rooms for two nights, while visiting his brother, just days before he murdered Abraham Lincoln in Washington. At the foot of Beacon Hill, the hotel has witnessed the comings and goings of both the influential and the notorious, including presidents and world leaders. In the early twentieth century, a young Malcolm Little (who later became Malcolm X) could be found working in the restaurant as a busboy, and Ho Chi Minh (the future Vietnamese Communist leader) was in the kitchen wearing a baker's hat for two years.

But none of the historical figures associated with the Parker were as important to American spirituality and religious life as Emerson. Born in 1803 in Boston, Emerson died in 1882 in his beloved Concord, his life spanning most of the nineteenth century. By the time he was presiding over the Saturday Club, Emerson had become the most important intellectual figure in America. Publishing his first essay at the age of thirty-three, the benignly titled *Nature* sparked the beginning of a movement, a rupture with his Unitarianism, that would later be called Transcendentalism, and the start of a slow dismantling of the doctrinal edifice that was Christianity before Darwin's *Origin of Species*, before Renan's *Life of Jesus*, indeed, before modernism had touched western religion itself.

Nature was written by a man who had already prepared for, and left behind, his chosen and almost predestined profession—that of clergyman. He'd succeeded at following in his father's footsteps, entering the Christian ministry, after a mediocre career in school, college, and seminary. Then, at twenty-five, he married the woman he adored, Ellen Tucker, only to lose her to tuberculosis two years later, which devastated him. Emerson's best biographer refers to this time in his life—of spiritual crisis and personal loss—as "his second birth."[5]

One year after Ellen's death, Emerson resigned his pastorate over the issue of Communion, saying that he could no longer, in good conscience, administer the sacrament. In the sermon preached before his congregation that day, Emerson said,

> *If I believed that [Communion] was enjoined by Jesus on his disciples, and that he even contemplated to make permanent this mode of commemoration . . . and yet on trial it was disagreeable to my own feelings, I should not adopt it.*[6]

This sermon marks the moment in which "Emerson becomes *Emerson*, the Emerson of the later essays who affirms the divinity of the self."[7] Soon after this, he was traveling throughout Europe; meeting the leading intellectual lights of his generation across the Atlantic (Wordsworth, Carlyle, Coleridge, etc.); reading philosophy, theology, and poetry in several languages; corresponding with the likes of Herman Grimm and Horace Greeley; becoming an interfaith trailblazer by exploring ideas from the East in the form of the Persian poet Hafiz and the Bhagavad-Gita;[8] and discovering the mature, confident, contrary, universalized "voice" that we now know as his.

The mature Emerson is focused always on the divinity of the individual. Harvard philosophy professor and author of *The Varieties of Religious Experience*, William James, spoke at the centenary of Emerson's birth in Concord on May 1903. He summarized Emerson's "voice" well:

> *The matchless eloquence with which Emerson proclaimed the sovereignty of the living individual electrified and emancipated his generation, and this bugle-blast*

will doubtless be regarded by future critics as the soul of
his message. The present man is the aboriginal reality,
the Institution is derivative, and the past man is irrele-
vant and obliterate for present issues.[9]

Many, however, resent Emerson for precisely the same reason:
for his elevation of the individual at the expense of dismantling
just about everything else. The biographer of Walker Percy, the
late twentieth-century novelist and Catholic convert who was
both drawn to and deeply resented Emerson's thought, expresses
this perspective well when describing Percy's view "that Emerson's was the mind most singly responsible for legitimizing the
abandonment of tradition, history, and even society in the name
of the imperial Self and the pursuit of happiness."[10]

TRANSCENDENTALISM AND EMERSON

The figure of Emerson may loom large over American cultural
life in the nineteenth century, but the views expressed throughout his writings are most associated with one specific literary,
spiritual, and philosophical movement known as Transcendentalism. Emerson was Transcendentalism's most public figure as
well as America's most visible intellectual; and he both embraced
and rejected the term, which did not originate with him.

The Transcendentalist movement began in the late 1820s and
early 1830s in and around Boston, among a handful of Harvard graduates who were dissatisfied with the intellectualism
of religious life, embodied in Unitarianism. Unitarianism itself
had begun as a response to the founding faith of the American
colonies: Puritanism, carried to the shores of the New World by
Pilgrims. And Puritanism had been primarily a departure from
English Anglicanism.

The Puritan faith was built upon a Calvinist foundation of
certain, divine revelation. Biblical truth was an assumption more
thoroughgoing and powerful than it had ever been for a Christian community, even going back to the Middle Ages, when few

people even read the Bible. So when the Enlightenment took hold, it failed to do so within Puritanism. This is when intellectually uneasy, progressive-leaning Puritans found an easy exit to Unitarianism—a movement that first sparked in the American colonies in Boston at the Anglican King's Chapel (across the street from the Parker House Hotel) in 1784.

So Unitarianism in America began, as it had earlier in Eastern Europe and England, as an intellectual reform movement, a difference of doctrine. Their signal belief was a rediscovery of Christian monotheism, dismantling the edifice of the Trinity, and a weakened view of Jesus Christ, usually regarding him to have been something less than God. At the same time, Unitarianism tended to retain much of the ethical and practical self-restraint and morality of their Puritan fathers, mothers, and friends. By about 1830, the first Transcendentalists became dissatisfied with both of these things. There was a sense among them that the asceticism of the Pilgrims—their sense of Christian duty, destiny, and hardship—had simply been outgrown in the New World. With firm roots now planted, the land was seen to be spiritually fertile, in and of itself, but still unnecessarily hindered by rationalism and *duty*. They sought to unhinge faith, to set it free from divine grace, allowing it to grow in a verdant, more mysterious, unpredictable environment unknown to earlier American generations.

From prominent pulpits in Boston, the Unitarian preacher William Ellery Channing (1780–1842) began to give Americans the notion of divinity of all people, an enhancement of the *imago Dei* stated in the Book of Genesis, God in us, a "likeness to God," in stark contrast to the Puritans' innate sinfulness and evil of human nature. Emerson took up this notion and expanded it, finding the Divine throughout the created world, not only in the hearts of men. Others, too, trumpeted these ideas. The quixotic Orestes Augustus Brownson, for instance, was espousing many Transcendentalist ideas at the same time as Emerson, from pulpits and in print, but his unpredictable nature and shocking conversion in 1844 to Roman Catholicism kept Brownson from having anything approaching the impact that Emerson would have on that first generation. It was Emerson's combination of affability, determination, and idealism that led to him being the leader of the movement.

The name Transcendentalist was coined by the movement's detractors because it sounded somewhat foolish, as well as foreign/German.[11] But the name is also apt, as it is a shorthand reference to the Transcendental Idealism of German philosopher Immanuel Kant. Kant believed (contra John Locke, whose views then dominated the English-speaking world) that things cannot be known to us in and of themselves, but the world is known to us only in how we perceive it. For the Transcendentalists, this meant that the only way of knowing the Divine, as well as truth, is by intuition and experience, in the natural, created world, rather than through the special providence of revealed religion. Following Kant instead of Locke, Emerson believed that every human mind is imbued with a divine instinct, an intuition toward apprehending *higher* ideas than what comes purely and simply through the normal activity of the senses. This the Transcendentalists called *reason*, in contrast to what the century before had been limited purely to *understanding*. And here comes the prime principle of the Transcendentalist movement: the divinity inside every person, too, often goes untapped.

Most Christians had retained the notion of revelation, the idea that there were certain truths revealed by God in the Bible that stand *outside* any normal ways of human knowledge, regardless of what Locke or anyone else had to say. But whereas Unitarianism had mostly jettisoned revelation, Transcendentalism actually set out to expand it. As Emerson puts it in the opening essay of his first essay collection,

> *We distinguish the announcements of the soul, its manifestations of its own nature, by the term "Revelation."*

*These are always attended by the emotion of the sub-
lime. For this communication is an influx of the Divine
mind into our mind. ("The Over-Soul," Essays: First)*

He couldn't put it much more emphatically than that.

When Emerson addressed the six graduates of Harvard's
Divinity College in 1838, he was asked to speak about theism.
The talk (see excerpts from the "Divinity School Address," below)
that resulted reverberated throughout New England and then
the world. Some called his revisions of theism, atheism, while
Emerson thought he was saving a living God from the heap of
Christian belief that dwelled too much on revelation "long ago
given and done, as if God were dead." Others regarded it as
German idealism made American. But to Emerson, the "Divin-
ity School Address" was the result of long struggles, like Jacob
wrestling with the angel all night long. This passage from his
October 1836 journal summarizes the perspective well:

*Oct. 19. As long as the soul seeks an external God, it
never can have peace, it always must be uncertain what
may be done & what may become of it. But when it sees
the Great God far within its own nature, then it sees
that always itself is a party to all that can be, that always
it will be informed of that which will happen and therefore it is pervaded with a great Peace.*[12]

Divine exclusivity in the mission, teachings, and person of
Jesus Christ were jettisoned, too—this time by both Unitarians
and Transcendentalists. Christian orthodoxy was dismantled.
This is why, as a young poet and Catholic convert who also
attended Harvard College, Robert Lowell expressed disgust in
a poem titled, "Concord." Referring to the belfry of a Unitarian
church, he writes with bitter irony that it "Clangs with preposterous torpor." The city of Concord itself is described as "where
Thoreau/And Emerson fleeced Heaven of Christ's robe."[13]

At the same time, some of traditional Christian teaching was repurposed, redefined. Miracles were just as wonderful as ever, but also entirely natural and common. Emerson asked his readers to imagine and see the miraculous all around them. In one of the most epigrammatic Emerson quotes of all, he states in *Nature*:

> *Why should we not also enjoy an original relation to the universe? Why should we not have a poetry and philosophy of insight and not of tradition, and a religion by revelation to us, and not the history of theirs?*

In some of these ways, Emerson stands in a long line of Christian thinkers, mystics, and practical theologians who have sought divine revelation outside the scriptures, viewed the human person as of noble and divine potential, and regarded the stuff of the earth itself as soil for these holy pursuits. I would place Francis of Assisi and his late medieval "Canticle of the Creatures" in the eddies of this stream, as well as Erasmus's Renaissance critique of religion, *Praise of Folly*. Even such an unimpeachable source within orthodox Christendom as the English poet and preacher John Donne produced passages such as this, which would have inspired Emerson as he imagined himself stepping outside of Christianity:

> *Wilt thou love God, as he thee? then digest,*
> *My soul, this wholesome meditation,*
> *How God the Spirit, by angels waited on*
> *In heaven, doth make his temple in thy breast.*
> *(Donne, "Divine Meditations," XV)*

Where Emerson really steps outside of Christian orthodoxy, in contrast to the others mentioned above, is when he sets nature beside the person of Christ as a source of divine revelation:

*The aspect of Nature is devout. Like the figure of Jesus,
she stands with bended head, and hands folded upon the
breast. The happiest man is he who learns from nature
the lesson of worship. ("Spirit," Nature)*

HIS INFLUENCE ON AMERICAN SPIRITUALITY

Emerson was the leader of what F. O. Matthiessen has called
the American Renaissance. He was the teacher, preacher, and
inspiration for the work of many of the luminaries that comprise
the syllabus of mid–nineteenth-century American literature:
Walt Whitman, Henry David Thoreau, Nathaniel Hawthorne,
Margaret Fuller, and Louisa May Alcott among them. William
James referred to Emerson on the centenary of his birth as the
voice that "rises strong and clear above the uproar of the times,
and seems securely destined to exert an ennobling influence over
future generations."[14]

More recently, Arthur Versluis has described Emerson as
America's most pivotal early leader (or guru) of *immediatism*,
which he defines as "spontaneous, direct, unmediated spiritual
insight into reality."[15] This, Emerson often claimed for himself,
as poet and seer of the divine in the human. He was self-consciously claiming what William Wordsworth had claimed a
generation earlier in England. Literary critic Harold Bloom has
made similar claims for Emerson's role in the history of American religion, and Emerson's metaphysical, meditative perspective on life and living have recently led some to draw a thread
of influence from his work to that of the twenty-first century
Protestant literary novelist Marilynne Robinson.[16]

Not everyone was thrilled, however, least of all his former
Unitarian brethren, by Emerson's radical new spiritual ideas.
Twenty-one years after the "Divinity School Address" of 1838
began the rumble, the American Unitarian Association saw fit to
state the following in its executive committee report. Emerson

was fifty years old, at the height of his influence throughout New England and beyond.

> *We desire, in a denominational capacity, to assert our profound belief in the Divine origin, the Divine authority, the Divine sanctions of the religion of Jesus Christ. . . . We desire openly to declare and record our belief as a denomination, so far as it can be officially represented . . . that God, moved by his own love, did raise up Jesus to aid in our redemption from sin, did by him pour a fresh flood of purifying life through the withered veins of humanity and along the corrupted channels of the world, and is, by his religion, forever sweeping the nations with regenerating gales from heaven, and visiting the hearts of men with celestial solicitations. We receive the teachings of Christ, separated from all foreign admixtures and later accretions, as infallible truth from God.*[17]

"In a denominational capacity" indeed! As an ecclesiastical body, Unitarians desired to remain distinctively Christian after their former son had clearly left the fold for broader pastures, but this is because many were already looking beyond their pews, listening to what Emerson and others inspired by him had to say.

Emerson had many admirers, in both the United States and abroad. He was one of the few American thinkers of the nineteenth century whose works were readily exported, read, discussed, and praised throughout the capitals of Europe. During his lifetime, continental admirers included the Bohemian poet Rainer Maria Rilke, the British-born but mostly Italian poet and painter Dante Gabriel Rossetti, and the notorious German philosopher Friedrich Nietzsche.

His influence is still felt today, even when it goes unnamed or uncredited. The very notion that there are universal ways of describing the character and spiritual composition of human beings can be traced back to Emerson. And there are authors

and spiritual teachers who have in recent years revived this
way of discourse, such as Paulo Coehlo, Deepak Chopra, Mark
Nepo, and Rob Bell, with stunning success. In work such as
theirs, Emerson lives in our own day.

PRAGMATISTS RESPOND

But immediately upon his death, critics began to dethrone him,
often on the charge of improper credentials. Emerson wasn't a
philosopher with training in the academy. He was more of a sage
and prophet than a critical thinker. In this regard, Walt Whitman
didn't help his friend's cause when he said, believing it a compliment, "[Emerson] may be obscure, but he is certain." Similarly,
Edgar Allan Poe, without the camaraderie, called Emerson's
writing "bad, sprawling, illegible, and irregular—although suf-
ficiently bold."[18] (Emerson was critical, in kind, of Poe's work.)
Overall, Emerson was seen as a writer who never lost his desire
to preach, despite the change in convictions. There is something
to these charges; they are not unfounded; and they were quite
effective in attaching themselves to Emerson's reputation then,
and even following him into our own century.

John Dewey, the great pragmatist and educational reformer,
was an early one to voice such concerns, in 1903 at a centennial
celebration for Emerson's birth; however, he did so in the context of praising Emerson as a champion of democracy as well as
"the one citizen of the New World fit to have his name uttered
in the same breath with that of Plato."[19] It was the Harvard
philosopher George Santayana who, three years earlier, in 1900,
attacked the credentials and standing of the Sage of Concord.
Santayana's tone is unmistakably cynical:

> Those who knew Emerson, or who stood so near to his
> time and to his circle that they caught some echo of his
> personal influence [this would have included Santayana
> himself], did not judge him merely as a poet or philos-
> opher, nor identify his efficacy with that of his writings.

> . . .[A]ll agreed in a veneration of his person which had nothing to do with their understanding or acceptance of his opinions. They flocked to him and listened to his word, not so much for the sake of its absolute meaning as for the atmosphere of candor, purity, and serenity that hung about it, as about a sort of sacred music. They felt themselves in the presence of a rare and beautiful spirit, who was in communion with a higher world.

He is also wrong.

This was not the usual response among audiences to Emerson, nor the reception of Emerson's ideas, which were widely challenged and debated throughout the nineteenth century. However, such talk created the straw man Santayana required in order to knock over Emerson with the charge that he wasn't a true philosopher; he couldn't say with precision what he meant by "Spirit" or the "Over-Soul," Santayana charged. And perhaps he was a man of some sort of wisdom but not a critical thinker. Santayana goes on to refer to Emerson's mind as "a fairyland of thoughts and fancies." He was a mystic, Santayana says, but he meant it as no compliment, for he defines mysticism as "the surrender of a category of thought because we divine its relativity."[20] To this day, this is the dominant opinion of professional philosophy regarding Emerson. He was once, however, a lightning rod figure in the philosophical tradition in the same way that Nietzsche was, even though Nietzsche survived similar charges, embraced by most of those on the *inside*. Nietzsche, in fact, credited Emerson as one of the most important influences on his own thought. He referred often to Emerson in his writings, both published and private, calling him a "master of prose" as well as "a brother soul."[21] To this day, few students study Emerson in philosophy class, but as John Dewey says earlier in the lecture quoted above, "Plato's own generation would, I think, have found it difficult to class Plato."[22]

EMERSON VS. THOREAU

So, Emerson wasn't a philosopher. And he wasn't yet what we've only in the last century come to call a *nature writer*. So what was he, exactly? Despite an undeniable historical prominence, Emerson often seems to strangely function in the American literary imagination as a John the Baptist to the more easily grasped, iconic, and somewhat mythological Henry David Thoreau. How the student is sometimes more popular than the teacher!

I would be the last to avert any reader's attention away from the ideas, writings, and man of Emerson's protégé. Like many, I, too, admired Thoreau first. But perhaps the contradiction is resolved by acknowledging that Thoreau is easily a hero, while Emerson is too expansive to be. Thoreau wrote one great book; it became great after his death, due, in large part, to the trumpeting of it by Emerson; but when I feel I have understood the man who built the cabin on Walden Pond, I think that I will continue to find fresh nuances in the varied ideas and enthusiasms of the Sage of Concord.

Emerson's and Thoreau's popular personas were so different that we are easily confused into supposing that Emerson was a settled, comfortable man, while Thoreau was the intrepid pioneer. In reality, most of Thoreau's ideas had their first expressions and origins in the writings of his teacher. Henry James once wrote,

> *The best things come . . . from the talents that are members of a group; every man works better when he has companions working in the same line, and yielding to the stimulus of suggestion, comparison, emulation. Great things have of course been done with double the pains they would have cost if they had been produced in more genial circumstances. The solitary worker loses the profit of example and discussion; he is apt to make*

> *awkward experiments; he is in the nature of the case
> more or less of an empiric.*[23]

He was writing about Nathaniel Hawthorne, suggesting that Hawthorne was one of those solitary thinkers, taking a more arduous, original path than do "members of a group." I doubt Hawthorne truly was; in fact, I doubt that anyone really is. Thoreau probably wasn't: he was indebted to Emerson—and others of their circle. In the years they shared, in fact, Thoreau was identified most often as a local crank who was dependent upon his generous mentor.

Even some of Thoreau's most famous lines were surely inspired by listening to Emerson. Compare, for instance, Thoreau's "I went to the woods because I wished to live deliberately, to front only the essential facts of life, and see if I could not learn what it had to teach, and not, when I came to die, discover that I had not lived" from *Walden; or, Life in the Woods* with "Life only avails, not the having lived," from Emerson's essay, "Self-Reliance." (Those who read "Self-Reliance" in Thoreau's lifetime were probably one thousand times the number who read *Walden*.)

Emerson became Thoreau's greatest champion, even publicist. Yet throughout the middle of the nineteenth century, there were half a dozen writers and thinkers from Concord who were more highly regarded and read than Thoreau—not just Emerson, but Hawthorne, Margaret Fuller, and in the decades after Thoreau's premature death, Louisa May Alcott. Today, however, it is Thoreau who most immediately appeals to a younger mind. For one thing, he died young and so seemingly lived most passionately. Secondly, he famously championed civil disobedience and passive resistance. He walked in the woods and lived deliberately. He sucked the marrow out of life. But the point is, he learned all of this from the long life of his mentor, who wrote and lectured about all of these things, albeit less with his boots on.

Finally, perhaps most important for Thoreau's easier popularity with younger and twenty-first century readers is his frequent use of the first person pronoun, *I*. This was also, incidentally, one way in which Walt Whitman (not to mention Emily Dickinson) took Emerson's ideas and personalized them for a wider audience, creating modern American lyric poetry along the way.

WAS HE TOO OPTIMISTIC?

If there is one final topic to address in an introduction to Emerson's spiritual writings, it is this: he is often criticized for his optimism regarding human nature. Critics say that he denied any reality to evil and that he failed to notice how the human heart reveals evidence of being far from divine. They point to instances such as the "Divinity School Address," when Emerson said, "Good is positive. Evil is merely privative, not absolute."

There are innumerable instances of this critique throughout the arts and in many fields of study. The most pointed and memorable may be John Williams's powerful novel about the American West, *Butcher's Crossing* (1960), which tells the story of Will Andrews, a third-year student at Harvard College, who leaves school in 1873 before taking a degree but after becoming well versed in Emerson's thought, seeking his own connection to nature. Journeying west, undergoing a variety of experiences, Will discovers that the natural world can be much less appealing than Emerson's idyllic vision. "At the gates of the forest, the surprised man of the world is forced to leave his city estimates of great and small, wise and foolish. The knapsack of custom falls off his back with the first step he takes into these precincts," Emerson wrote in *Nature*. But one doesn't have to believe in the Christian doctrine of original sin in order to observe how being "one with Nature" does not, in the end, provide an escape from what seems to be awful and recurring in *human* nature.[24] Will Andrews leaves college lecture halls with an innocence and purity that is then spoiled by directly confronting what Emerson described as glorious.

But there is also evidence to the contrary—to demonstrate that Emerson held a more balanced view of human nature. He, for instance, easily observed the frequent tendency and folly of prophets, theologians, and the self-consciously *spiritual*, to over-reach with what they believe and say. Witness this paragraph from "Nature" in *Essays: Second*:

> *No man is quite sane; each has a vein of folly in his com-*
> *position, a slight determination of blood to the head, to*
> *make sure of holding him hard to some one point which*
> *nature had taken to heart. Great causes are never tried*
> *on their merits; but the cause is reduced to particulars*
> *to suit the size of the partisans, and the contention is*
> *ever hottest on minor matters. Not less remarkable is*
> *the overfaith of each man in the importance of what*
> *he has to do or say. The poet, the prophet, has a higher*
> *value for what he utters than any hearer, and therefore it*
> *gets spoken. The strong, self-complacent Luther declares*
> *with an emphasis, not to be mistaken, that "God him-*
> *self cannot do without wise men." Jacob Behmen and*
> *George Fox betray their egotism in the pertinacity of*
> *their controversial tracts, and James Naylor once suf-*
> *fered himself to be worshipped as the Christ. Each*
> *prophet comes presently to identify himself with his*
> *thought, and to esteem his hat and shoes sacred. How-*
> *ever this may discredit such persons with the judicious,*
> *it helps them with the people, as it gives heat, pungency,*
> *and publicity to their words. A similar experience is not*
> *infrequent in private life. Each young and ardent person*
> *writes a diary, in which, when the hours of prayer and*
> *penitence arrive, he inscribes his soul. The pages thus*
> *written are, to him, burning and fragrant: he reads them*
> *on his knees by midnight and by the morning star; he*

wets them with his tears: they are sacred; too good for
the world, and hardly yet to be shown to the dearest
friend. This is the man-child that is born to the soul, and
her life still circulates in the babe. The umbilical cord
has not yet been cut.

This is why William James, correctly, I think, was able to say,
"[Emerson's] optimism had nothing in common with that indis-
criminate hurrahing for the Universe with which Walt Whitman
has made us familiar."[25]

ABOUT THIS COLLECTION OF WRITINGS

This book excerpts widely and discriminately from Emerson's
published writings, focusing on the spiritual themes. Anyone
who has read Emerson in school, and heard references to him in
literary and cultural histories, may not be cognizant of the fact
of Emerson's ideas as distinctively spiritual. The usual themes
associated with Emerson are self-reliance, individuality, nature,
universal brotherhood, and friendship. Lesser known are the
aspects of his thought that make him one of the modern spiritual masters.

I have identified five of these, weaving throughout his writings. They fall into the following groupings, each inspired by a
phrase from Emerson's work.

"Newborn Bards of the Holy Ghost"

From his famous Harvard Divinity School Commencement
address of 1838, this phrase captures the most essential tenets of
Emerson's spiritual vision. Lawrence Buell has called Emerson's
"Divinity School Address" his "most polished and celebrated
heretical discourse."[26] In it, individual expression is offered at
the expense of Unitarianism's creedal commitments. Emerson
wrote frequently of how all people should reach for individuality over conformity, and we find it measured and governed by

an invisible force, the unpredictable spirit of God. This phrase is also a prime example of how the spiritual language of Emerson is too often forgotten, or overshadowed, by his more humanistic writings; one could easily place some of what is in this section under the more familiar Emersonian heading of "Self-Reliance," yet I believe that that is to miss an important aspect of what the writer was attempting to communicate about the dramatic change of perspective and spirit required in order to enter into this new era. He was a seer, first and foremost.

"We Must Be Lovers"

Another title for this section might be "Throbbing Hearts," an image from one of Emerson's little-known poems included here. He often writes of human passion as the best measure of truth. In fact, heart and truth are among the words he uses most often. It was in this context that he brought the ideas of Hafiz and Sufism to the West as well as a desire to use Sufi principles as a corrective for New England Christianity. In this category, Emerson expresses himself in language that echoes the classic texts of the East that he was discovering. Consider this paragraph from a sermon he first delivered in 1831, five years before the pamphlet *Nature* would widely publicize his views on religion. His text for the week was Romans 14:5, "Let every man be fully persuaded in his own mind."

> [D]o not suppose, my friends, that in ceasing forever to act from a regard to our example and acting from simple regard to the good or the evil of the action itself, do not suppose that in so doing we should be relaxing the obligations to virtue. We should be coming under a more not less strict law. We have the dangerous habit of reading our duty in the eyes of others; and others judge by the false standard of custom; but if we will cast down this and every idol, and let God speak by his word and by his Representative in the human heart, and allow

*ourselves only in such freedom as that allows, and do
all which that enjoins, we shall find the day is not long
enough to leave us leisure, nor a saint's life pure enough
to satisfy its law.*[27]

Few of his readers would have known how imbued his words
were with the teachings of Hafiz and the Bhagavad-Gita.

"A Wise Skepticism"

The ancient Stoics were among the first philosopher–theologians
to point out that the natural world may be able to *tell* us all
that we really need to know. Emerson's easy acceptance of death
appears throughout his writings and was witnessed by his contemporaries in the bias he brought to editing Thoreau's letters in
1865. He wrote no introduction or notes to that volume, and did
not even attach his name to its publication, so it is not excerpted
here. However, Emerson showed his admiration for the Stoic
side of Thoreau with the letters he chose to include as well as
those he excluded. Twenty-nine years later, F. B. Sanborn issued
a new collection of the letters of Thoreau, whom Sanborn also
knew personally, deliberately adding to the earlier work many of
the letters Thoreau wrote to his sister and others, showing mirth,
cheerfulness, and joy. Sanborn wrote in the Introduction to his
1894 volume, "The selection made for a small volume in 1865
was designedly done to exhibit one phase of his character,—the
most striking, if you will, but not the most native or attractive."
The point being made was simple: there was more to Thoreau
than sensible sobriety, commitment to justice, and living deliberately, but Emerson most appreciated those famous aspects of the
friend he made famous. One finds these themes also, subtly but
profoundly, in his essays.

"Live in the Present"

A complicated man and thinker, Emerson occasionally seems to contradict himself, but while this theme may appear to be the opposite of stoicism (in the previous section), it is not. The ancient Stoics were different than the adjectival use of the word stoical denotes today, and there is a persistent theme of cultivating virtue in the writings of the ancient Stoics, as in Emerson's writings. Particularly later in life, he wrote often of ways to stimulate growth in the life of the soul, using frequent images of gardens and orchards. (He was himself, however, a less successful gardener than he was a wanderer across wide fields—and that is the reason for the final category.)

"Wise Ancient Woods"

This is the dreamer Emerson, as well as the experiential one. It is where earth meets heaven in his thought. More popularly associated with Thoreau, who exhibited wildness in his explorations of the natural world, Emerson was the inspiration for this very spiritual idea, not quite of rebellion, but radical independence and a celebration of the as-yet unknown. For example, Emerson summarized this perspective beautifully in two lines of a poem: "So nigh is grandeur to our dust,/So near is God to man!" All of these writings demonstrate the unique qualities of the working philosopher, community organizer, man of letters, and public intellectual. Harvard professor Lawrence Buell summarizes this best when he describes these writings possessing

> *a peculiar blend—of humility and assertiveness, sincerity and irony, abstraction and directness, intransigent position-taking versus infinite wariness about being pinned down to any one formulation—still remains the power to startle and excite, to produce unexpected flashes of insight.*[28]

A NOTE ABOUT THE TEXTS

Some spelling has been adjusted to reflect twenty-first century American English normative usage. For example, "Shakspeare" becomes "Shakespeare" and "to-day" becomes "today." No other changes have been made, including punctuation, and no attempt has been made to correct or smooth Emerson's idiosyncratic use of language, sudden use of obscure words, and occasional love for the second-person singular simple present form of certain verbs (e.g., "seest" for "see"). Archaic words such as "maugre" are also left alone. And from this point forward, for the sake of brevity, our author's name, Ralph Waldo Emerson, will be abbreviated to RWE in the editor's notes and remarks.

1

"Newborn Bards of the Holy Ghost" (After Christianity)

RWE was a poststructuralist before there was structuralism. He was a mystic discovering the religions of the East at a time when mystics were all considered Hindoos. He was a naturalist at a time when any expression of regard for the earth associated one with the unsophisticated. He broke with Christianity for reasons that have since become common, because he found it cold and rational, too bound to historic revelation, and without feeling or sensitivity to the Spirit. Those who followed him did so by also leaving the faith behind like a bear's den abandoned after a long winter. As a Christian myself, I often feel that I want RWE back. I would like to sit beside him in church pews and listen to where he diverges from what's traditionally acceptable. His creative vision still has the power to renew.

This opening section of readings is the first signpost of RWE's beliefs and teachings: on the natural divinity of humankind. As he wrote in his private journal in April 1840: "In all my lectures, I have taught one doctrine, namely, the infinitude of the private man. This, the people accept readily enough, & even with loud commendation, as long as I call the lecture, Art; or Politics; or Literature; or the Household; but the moment I call it Religion,—they are shocked, though it be only the application of the same truth which they receive everywhere else, to a new class of facts."[29]

"WE ARE BORN BELIEVING"

This selection comes from the latter works of RWE. It summa-
rizes well his perspective on what has happened to Christianity,
seeing it as a dead form of spiritual questing by the mid-nine-
teenth century. He also lays out his theory that religion can never
contain the Deity, or faith. From "Worship," Conduct.

We are born loyal. The whole creation is made of hooks and
eyes, of bitumen, of sticking-plaster, and whether your community is made in Jerusalem or in California, of saints or of wreck-
ers, it coheres in a perfect ball. Men as naturally make a state,
or a church, as caterpillars a web. If they were more refined, it
would be less formal, it would be nervous, like that of the Shakers, who, from long habit of thinking and feeling together, it is
said, are affected in the same way, at the same time, to work and
to play, and as they go with perfect sympathy to their tasks in
the field or shop, so are they inclined for a ride or a journey at
the same instant, and the horses come up with the family car-
riage unbespoken to the door.

We are born believing. A man bears beliefs, as a tree bears
apples. A self-poise belongs to every particle; and a rectitude to
every mind, and is the Nemesis and protector of every society. I
and my neighbors have been bred in the notion, that, unless we
came soon to some good church,—Calvinism, or Behmenism, or
Romanism, or Mormonism,—there would be a universal thaw
and dissolution. No Isaiah or Jeremy has arrived. Nothing can
exceed the anarchy that has followed in our skies. The stern old
faiths have all pulverized. 'Tis a whole population of gentlemen
and ladies out in search of religions. 'Tis as flat anarchy in our
ecclesiastic realms, as that which existed in Massachusetts, in
the Revolution, or which prevails now on the slope of the Rocky
Mountains or Pike's Peak. Yet we make shift to live. Men are
loyal. Nature has self-poise in all her works; certain proportions

in which oxygen and azote combine, and, not less a harmony in faculties, a fitness in the spring and the regulator.

The decline of the influence of Calvin, or Fenelon, or Wesley, or Channing, need give us no uneasiness. The builder of heaven has not so ill constructed his creature as that the religion, that is, the public nature, should fall out: the public and the private element, like north and south, like inside and outside, like centrifugal and centripetal, adhere to every soul, and cannot be subdued, except the soul is dissipated. God builds his temple in the heart on the ruins of churches and religions. . . .

There is always some religion, some hope and fear extended into the invisible,—from the blind boding which nails a horseshoe to the mast or the threshold, up to the song of the Elders in the Apocalypse. But the religion cannot rise above the state of the votary. Heaven always bears some proportion to earth. The god of the cannibals will be a cannibal, of the crusaders a crusader, and of the merchants a merchant. In all ages, souls out of time, extraordinary, prophetic, are born, who are rather related to the system of the world, than to their particular age and locality. These announce absolute truths, which, with whatever reverence received, are speedily dragged down into a savage interpretation. The interior tribes of our Indians, and some of the Pacific islanders, flog their gods, when things take an unfavorable turn. The Greek poets did not hesitate to let loose their petulant wit on their deities also. . . .

We live in a transition period, when the old faiths which comforted nations, and not only so, but made nations, seem to have spent their force. I do not find the religions of men at this moment very creditable to them, but either childish and insignificant, or unmanly and effeminating. The fatal trait is the divorce between religion and morality. Here are know-nothing religions, or churches that proscribe intellect; scortatory religions; slave-holding and slave-trading religions; and, even in the decent populations, idolatries wherein the whiteness of the ritual covers scarlet indulgence. The lover of the old religion complains that our contemporaries, scholars as well as merchants, succumb to a great despair,—have corrupted into a timorous conservatism, and believe in nothing. In our large cities, the population is god-less, materialized,—no bond, no fellow-feeling, no enthusiasm. These are not men, but hungers, thirsts, fevers, and appetites walking. How is it people manage to live on,—so aimless as they are? After their peppercorn aims are gained, it seems as if the lime in their bones alone held them together, and not any worthy purpose. There is no faith in the intellectual, none in the moral universe. There is faith in chemistry, in meat, and wine, in wealth, in machinery, in the steam engine, galvanic battery, turbine wheels, sewing machines, and in public opinion, but not in divine causes. A silent revolution has loosed the tension of the old religious sects, and, in place of the gravity and permanence of those societies of opinion, they run into freak and extrava-gance. In creeds never was such levity; witness the heathenisms in Christianity, the periodic "revivals," the Millennium mathemat-ics, the peacock ritualism, the retrogression to Popery, the maun-dering of Mormons, the squalor of Mesmerism, the deliration of rappings, the rat and mouse revelation, thumps in table-drawers, and black art. The architecture, the music, the prayer, partake of the madness: the arts sink into shift and make-believe. Not knowing what to do, we ape our ancestors; the churches stagger backward to the mummeries of the dark ages. By the irresist-ible maturing of the general mind, the Christian traditions have lost their hold. The dogma of the mystic offices of Christ being dropped, and he standing on his genius as a moral teacher, 'tis impossible to maintain the old emphasis of his personality; and it recedes, as all persons must, before the sublimity of the moral laws. From this change, and in the momentary absence of any religious genius that could offset the immense material activity, there is a feeling that religion is gone.

"FAITH MAKES US"

Here we have selections from the 1838 "Divinity School Address," RWE's most radical and challenging writing to establishment religion and faith. These stirring words were preached to an audience that included only six graduates of Harvard Divinity School seeking to enter Christian ministry, along with members of their families. As the Harvard scholar Lawrence Buell summarizes, "Harvard College and/or its divinity school" were, in those days, the "bastion and ministerial training ground for Unitarianism."[30] The liberal wing of Congregationalists had separated from the Puritans twenty-three years earlier. RWE was an ex-Unitarian minister. Some critics hear atheism in RWE's words. Above all, RWE urges the graduates to only preach what they come to know by personal experience. That way, they are able to become, each, a "newborn bard of the Holy Ghost."

[F]irst of all . . . go alone. [R]efuse the good models, even those which are sacred in the imagination of men, and dare to love God without mediator or veil. Friends enough you shall find who will hold up to your emulation Wesleys and Oberlins, Saints and Prophets. Thank God for these good men, but say, "I also am a man." Imitation cannot go above its model. The imitator dooms himself to hopeless mediocrity. The inventor did it, because it was natural to him, and so in him it has a charm. In the imitator, something else is natural, and he bereaves himself of his own beauty, to come short of another man's.

Yourself a newborn bard of the Holy Ghost,—cast behind you all conformity, and acquaint men at first hand with Deity. Look to it first and only, that fashion, custom, authority, pleasure, and money, are nothing to you,—are not bandages over your eyes, that you cannot see,—but live with the privilege of the immeasurable mind. Not too anxious to visit periodically all families and each family in your parish connection,—when you meet one of these men or women, be to them a divine man; be to them thought and virtue; let their timid aspirations find in you a friend; let their trampled instincts be genially tempted out in your atmosphere; let their doubts know that you have doubted, and their wonder feel that you have wondered. By trusting your own heart, you shall gain more confidence in other men. For all our penny-wisdom, for all our soul-destroying slavery to habit, it is not to be doubted, that all men have sublime thoughts; that all men value the few real hours of life; they love to be heard; they love to be caught up into the vision of principles. We mark with light in the memory the few interviews we have had, in the dreary years of routine and of sin, with souls that made our souls wiser; that spoke what we thought; that told us what we knew; that gave us leave to be what we inly were. Discharge to men the priestly office, and, present or absent, you shall be followed with their love as by an angel.

And, to this end, let us not aim at common degrees of merit. Can we not leave, to such as love it, the virtue that glitters for the commendation of society, and ourselves pierce the deep solitudes of absolute ability and worth? We easily come up to the standard of goodness in society. Society's praise can be cheaply secured, and almost all men are content with those easy merits; but the instant effect of conversing with God, will be, to put them away. There are persons who are not actors, not speakers, but influences; persons too great for fame, for display; who disdain eloquence; to whom all we call art and artist, seems too nearly allied to show and by-ends, to the exaggeration of the finite and selfish, and loss of the universal. The orators, the poets, the commanders encroach on us only as fair women do, by our allowance and homage. Slight them by preoccupation of mind, slight them, as you can well afford to do, by high and universal aims, and they instantly feel that you have right, and that it is in lower places that they must shine. They also feel your right; for they with you are open to the influx of the all-knowing

Spirit, which annihilates before its broad noon the little shades and gradations of intelligence in the compositions we call wiser and wisest.

In such high communion, let us study the grand strokes of rectitude: a bold benevolence, an independence of friends, so that not the unjust wishes of those who love us, shall impair our freedom, but we shall resist for truth's sake the freest flow of kindness, and appeal to sympathies far in advance; and,— what is the highest form in which we know this beautiful element,—a certain solidity of merit, that has nothing to do with opinion, and which is so essentially and manifestly virtue, that it is taken for granted, that the right, the brave, the generous step will be taken by it, and nobody thinks of commending it. You would compliment a coxcomb doing a good act, but you would not praise an angel. The silence that accepts merit as the most natural thing in the world is the highest applause. Such souls, when they appear, are the Imperial Guard of Virtue, the perpetual reserve, the dictators of fortune. One needs not praise their courage,—they are the heart and soul of nature. O my friends, there are resources in us on which we have not drawn. There are men who rise refreshed on hearing a threat; men to whom a crisis which intimidates and paralyzes the majority,—demanding not the faculties of prudence and thrift, but comprehension, immovableness, the readiness of sacrifice,—comes graceful and beloved as a bride. Napoleon said of Massena, that he was not himself until the battle began to go against him; then, when the dead began to fall in ranks around him, awoke his powers of combination, and he put on terror and victory as a robe. So it is in rugged crises, in unweariable endurance, and in aims which put sympathy out of question, that the angel is shown. But these are heights that we can scarce remember and look up to, without contrition and shame. Let us thank God that such things exist.

And now let us do what we can to rekindle the smouldering, nigh quenched fire on the altar. The evils of the church that

now is are manifest. The question returns, What shall we do? I
confess, all attempts to project and establish a Cultus with new
rites and forms, seem to me vain. Faith makes us, and not we it,
and faith makes its own forms. All attempts to contrive a system
are as cold as the new worship introduced by the French to the
goddess of Reason,—today, pasteboard and filigree, and ending
tomorrow in madness and murder. Rather let the breath of new
life be breathed by you through the forms already existing. For,
if once you are alive, you shall find they shall become plastic and
new. The remedy to their deformity is, first, soul, and second,
soul, and evermore, soul. A whole popedom of forms, one pulsa-
tion of virtue can uplift and vivify. Two inestimable advantages
Christianity has given us; first; the Sabbath, the jubilee of the
whole world; whose light dawns welcome alike into the closet
of the philosopher, into the garret of toil, and into prison cells,
and everywhere suggests, even to the vile, the dignity of spiritual being. Let it stand forevermore, a temple, which new love,
new faith, new sight shall restore to more than its first splendor to mankind. And secondly, the institution of preaching,—
the speech of man to men,—essentially the most flexible of all
organs, of all forms. What hinders that now, everywhere, in pulpits, in lecture-rooms, in houses, in fields, wherever the invitation of men or your own occasions lead you, you speak the very
truth, as your life and conscience teach it, and cheer the waiting,
fainting hearts of men with new hope and new revelation?

I look for the hour when that supreme Beauty, which ravished
the souls of those eastern men, and chiefly of those Hebrews,
and through their lips spoke oracles to all time, shall speak in the
West also. The Hebrew and Greek Scriptures contain immortal
sentences, that have been bread of life to millions. But they have
no epical integrity; are fragmentary; are not shown in their order
to the intellect. I look for the new Teacher, that shall follow so
far those shining laws, that he shall see them come full circle;
shall see their rounding complete grace; shall see the world to be

the mirror of the soul; shall see the identity of the law of gravitation with purity of heart; and shall show that the Ought, that Duty, is one thing with Science, with Beauty, and with Joy.

"OUR YOUNG PEOPLE ARE DISEASED WITH . . . THEOLOGICAL PROBLEMS"

In this passage from the essay, "Spiritual Laws," RWE explains how the intellectual life, learning, book, and theological speculation often work against a person's natural, divinely inspired, understanding. This is one of his strongest manifestos of what we might today call "spirituality over religion."

When the act of reflection takes place in the mind, when we look at ourselves in the light of thought, we discover that our life is embosomed in beauty. Behind us, as we go, all things assume pleasing forms, as clouds do far off. Not only things familiar and stale, but even the tragic and terrible, are comely, as they take their place in the pictures of memory. The riverbank, the weed at the water-side, the old house, the foolish person,—however neglected in the passing,—have a grace in the past. Even the corpse that has lain in the chambers has added a solemn ornament to the house. The soul will not know either deformity or pain. If, in the hours of clear reason, we should speak the severest truth, we should say, that we had never made a sacrifice. In these hours the mind seems so great, that nothing can be taken from us that seems much. All loss, all pain, is particular; the universe remains to the heart unhurt. Neither vexations nor calamities abate our trust. No man ever stated his griefs as lightly as he might. Allow for exaggeration in the most patient and sorely ridden hack that ever was driven. For it is only the finite that has wrought and suffered; the infinite lies stretched in smiling repose.

The intellectual life may be kept clean and healthful, if man will live the life of nature, and not import into his mind difficulties which are none of his. No man need be perplexed in his speculations. Let him do and say what strictly belongs to him, and, though very ignorant of books, his nature shall not yield him any intellectual obstructions and doubts. Our young people are diseased with the theological problems of original sin, origin of evil, predestination, and the like. These never presented a practical difficulty to any man,—never darkened across any man's road, who did not go out of his way to seek them. These are the soul's mumps, and measles, and whooping coughs, and those who have not caught them cannot describe their health or prescribe the cure. A simple mind will not know these enemies. It is quite another thing that he should be able to give account of his faith, and expound to another the theory of his self-union and freedom. This requires rare gifts. Yet, without this self-knowledge, there may be a sylvan strength and integrity in that which he is. "A few strong instincts and a few plain rules" suffice us.

My will never gave the images in my mind the rank they now take. The regular course of studies, the years of academic and professional education, have not yielded me better facts than some idle books under the bench at the Latin School. What we do not call education is more precious than that which we call so. We form no guess, at the time of receiving a thought, of its comparative value. And education often wastes its effort in attempts to thwart and balk this natural magnetism, which is sure to select what belongs to it.

In like manner, our moral nature is vitiated by any interference of our will. People represent virtue as a struggle, and take to themselves great airs upon their attainments, and the question is everywhere vexed, when a noble nature is commended, whether the man is not better who strives with temptation. But there is no merit in the matter. Either God is there, or he is not there. We love characters in proportion as they are impulsive and spontaneous. The less a man thinks or knows about his virtues, the better we like him. Timoleon's victories are the best victories;

which ran and flowed like Homer's verses, Plutarch said. When we see a soul whose acts are all regal, graceful, and pleasant as roses, we must thank God that such things can be and are, and not turn sourly on the angel, and say, "Crump is a better man with his grunting resistance to all his native devils."

Not less conspicuous is the preponderance of nature over will in all practical life. There is less intention in history than we ascribe to it. We impute deep-laid, far-sighted plans to Caesar and Napoleon; but the best of their power was in nature, not in them. Men of an extraordinary success, in their honest moments, have always sung, "Not unto us, not unto us." According to the faith of their times, they have built altars to Fortune, or to Destiny, or to St. Julian. Their success lay in their parallelism to the course of thought, which found in them an unobstructed channel; and the wonders of which they were the visible conductors seemed to the eye their deed. Did the wires generate the galvanism? It is even true that there was less in them on which they could reflect, than in another; as the virtue of a pipe is to be smooth and hollow. That which externally seemed will and immovableness was willingness and self-annihilation. Could Shakespeare give a theory of Shakespeare? Could ever a man of prodigious mathematical genius convey to others any insight into his methods? If he could communicate that secret, it would instantly lose its exaggerated value, blending with the daylight and the vital energy the power to stand and to go.

The lesson is forcibly taught by these observations, that our life might be much easier and simpler than we make it; that the world might be a happier place than it is; that there is no need of struggles, convulsions, and despairs, of the wringing of the hands and the gnashing of the teeth; that we miscreate our own evils. We interfere with the optimism of nature; for, whenever we get this vantage-ground of the past, or of a wiser mind in the present, we are able to discern that we are begirt with laws which execute themselves.

The face of external nature teaches the same lesson. Nature will not have us fret and fume. She does not like our benevolence or our learning much better than she likes our frauds and wars. When we come out of the caucus, or the bank, or the Abolition-convention, or the Temperance-meeting, or the Transcendental club, into the fields and woods, she says to us, "So hot? my little Sir."

We are full of mechanical actions. We must needs intermeddle, and have things in our own way, until the sacrifices and virtues of society are odious. Love should make joy; but our benevolence is unhappy. Our Sunday schools, and churches, and pauper-societies are yokes to the neck. We pain ourselves to please nobody. There are natural ways of arriving at the same ends at which these aim, but do not arrive. Why should all virtue work in one and the same way? Why should all give dollars? It is very inconvenient to us country folk, and we do not think any good will come of it. We have not dollars; merchants have; let them give them. Farmers will give corn; poets will sing; women will sew; laborers will lend a hand; the children will bring flowers. And why drag this dead weight of a Sunday school over the whole Christendom? It is natural and beautiful that childhood should inquire, and maturity should teach; but it is time enough to answer questions when they are asked. Do not shut up the young people against their will in a pew, and force the children to ask them questions for an hour against their will.

If we look wider, things are all alike; laws, and letters, and creeds, and modes of living, seem a travesty of truth. Our society is encumbered by ponderous machinery, which resembles the endless aqueducts which the Romans built over hill and dale, and which are superseded by the discovery of the law that water rises to the level of its source. It is a Chinese wall which any nimble Tartar can leap over. It is a standing army, not so good as a peace. It is a graduated, titled, richly appointed empire, quite superfluous when town meetings are found to answer just as well.

Let us draw a lesson from nature, which always works by short ways. When the fruit is ripe, it falls. When the fruit is dispatched, the leaf falls. The circuit of the waters is mere falling. The walking of man and all animals is a falling forward. All our manual labor and works of strength, as prying, splitting, digging, rowing, and so forth, are done by dint of continual falling, and the globe, earth, moon, comet, sun, star, fall for ever and ever.

"OLD FORMS OF RELIGION DECAY"

Continuing the theme of the last excerpt, this portion of a paragraph is from the essay "Worship," Conduct.

We say, the old forms of religion decay, and that a skepticism devastates the community. I do not think it can be cured or stayed by any modification of theologic creeds, much less by theologic discipline. The cure for false theology is motherwit. Forget your books and traditions, and obey your moral perceptions at this hour. That which is signified by the words "moral" and "spiritual," is a lasting essence, and, with whatever illusions we have loaded them, will certainly bring back the words, age after age, to their ancient meaning. I know no words that mean so much. In our definitions, we grope after the spiritual by describing it as invisible. The true meaning of spiritual is real; that law which executes itself, which works without means, and which cannot be conceived as not existing. Men talk of "mere morality,"— which is much as if one should say "poor God, with nobody to help him." I find the omnipresence and the almightiness in the reaction of every atom in Nature.

"CONTRAST[ING] THE CHURCH WITH THE SOUL"

Aphorisms abound in this signal long paragraph from the "Divinity School Address." This is a fine example of what

*Robert D. Richardson refers to as the "optative ebullience" and
"metaphorical panache" in RWE's writing.*[31]

And now, my brothers, you will ask, What in these despond-
ing days can be done by us? The remedy is already declared in
the ground of our complaint of the Church. We have contrasted
the Church with the Soul. In the soul, then, let the redemption
be sought. Wherever a man comes, there comes revolution. The
old is for slaves. When a man comes, all books are legible, all
things transparent, all religions are forms. He is religious. Man
is the wonderworker. He is seen amid miracles. All men bless
and curse. He saith yea and nay, only. The stationariness of religion; the assumption that the age of inspiration is past, that the
Bible is closed; the fear of degrading the character of Jesus by
representing him as a man; indicate with sufficient clearness
the falsehood of our theology. It is the office of a true teacher
to show us that God is, not was; that He speaketh, not spake.
The true Christianity,—a faith like Christ's in the infinitude of
man,—is lost. None believeth in the soul of man, but only in
some man or person old and departed. Ah me! no man goeth
alone. All men go in flocks to this saint or that poet, avoiding
the God who seeth in secret. They cannot see in secret; they love
to be blind in public. They think society wiser than their soul,
and know not that one soul, and their soul, is wiser than the
whole world. See how nations and races flit by on the sea of
time, and leave no ripple to tell where they floated or sunk, and
one good soul shall make the name of Moses, or of Zeno, or of
Zoroaster, reverend forever. None assayeth the stern ambition
to be the Self of the nation, and of nature, but each would be an
easy secondary to some Christian scheme, or sectarian connection, or some eminent man. Once leave your own knowledge of
God, your own sentiment, and take secondary knowledge, as St.
Paul's, or George Fox's, or Swedenborg's, and you get wide from
God with every year this secondary form lasts, and if, as now,

for centuries,—the chasm yawns to that breadth, that men can scarcely be convinced there is in them anything divine.

"THE PROBLEM" (POEM)

RWE was considered one of his country's most important poets, and this poem expresses his religious and spiritual priorities as they were rapidly evolving in the late 1830s. From Early Poems.

> I like a church, I like a cowl,
> I love a prophet of the soul,
>
> And on my heart monastic aisles
> Fall like sweet strains or pensive smiles;
> Yet not for all his faith can see,
> Would I that cowled churchman be.
> Why should the vest on him allure,
> Which I could not on me endure?
>
> Not from a vain or shallow thought
> His awful Jove young Phidias brought;
> Never from lips of cunning fell
> The thrilling Delphic oracle;
> Out from the heart of nature rolled
> The burdens of the Bible old;
> The litanies of nations came,
> Like the volcano's tongue of flame,
> Up from the burning core below,
> The canticles of love and woe.
> The hand that rounded Peter's dome,
> And groined the aisles of Christian Rome,
> Wrought in a sad sincerity,
> Himself from God he could not free;

He builded better than he knew,
The conscious stone to beauty grew.

Know'st thou what wove yon woodbird's nest
Of leaves and feathers from her breast;
Or how the fish outbuilt its shell,
Painting with morn each annual cell;
Or how the sacred pine tree adds
To her old leaves new myriads?
Such and so grew these holy piles,
Whilst love and terror laid the tiles.
Earth proudly wears the Parthenon
As the best gem upon her zone;
And Morning opes with haste her lids
To gaze upon the Pyramids;
O'er England's abbeys bends the sky
As on its friends with kindred eye;
For out of Thought's interior sphere
These wonders rose to upper air,
And nature gladly gave them place,
Adopted them into her race,
And granted them an equal date
With Andes and with Ararat.

These temples grew as grows the grass,
Art might obey but not surpass.
The passive Master lent his hand
To the vast soul that o'er him planned,
And the same power that reared the shrine,
Bestrode the tribes that knelt within.
Even the fiery Pentecost
Girds with one flame the Countless host,
Trances the heart through chanting quires,
And through the priest the mind inspires.

The word unto the prophet spoken
Was writ on tables yet unbroken;
The word by seers or sibyls told
In groves of oak, or fanes of gold,
Still floats upon the morning wind,
Still whispers to the willing mind.
One accent of the Holy Ghost
The heedless world hath never lost.

I know what say the Fathers wise,
The Book itself before me lies,
Old Chrysostom, best Augustine,
And he who blent both in his line,
The younger Golden-lips or mines,
Taylor, the Shakspeare of divines,
His words are music in my ear,
I see his cowled portrait dear,
And yet for all his faith could see,
I would not the good bishop be.

"OUR TORMENT IS UNBELIEF"

A short selection from a lecture delivered in December 1841.

A new disease has fallen on the life of man. Every Age, like every
human body, has its own distemper. Other times have had war,
or famine, or a barbarism domestic or bordering, as their antag-
onism. Our forefathers walked in the world and went to their
graves, tormented with the fear of Sin, and the terror of the Day
of Judgment. These terrors have lost their force, and our tor-
ment is Unbelief, the Uncertainty as to what we ought to do;
the distrust of the value of what we do, and the distrust that
the Necessity (which we all at last believe in) is fair and benefi-
cent. Our Religion assumes the negative form of rejection. Out
of love of the true, we repudiate the false: and the Religion is an

abolishing criticism. A great perplexity hangs like a cloud on the brow of all cultivated persons, a certain imbecility in the best spirits, which distinguishes the period. We do not find the same trait in the Arabian, in the Hebrew, in Greek, Roman, Norman, English periods; no, but in other men a natural firmness. The men did not see beyond the need of the hour. They planted their foot strong, and doubted nothing. We mistrust every step we take. We find it the worst thing about time, that we know not what to do with it.

"INSPIRED BY THE DIVINE SOUL"

This is from an address delivered before the Phi Beta Kappa Society, Harvard College, Cambridge, Massachusetts, on August 31, 1837. It reminds me of what Robert Frost once said about the complicated ideas so often present in RWE's writing: "I don't like obscurity and obfuscation, but I do like dark sayings I must leave the clearing of to time. And I don't want to be robbed of the pleasure of fathoming depths for myself."[32]

It is one of those fables which, out of an unknown antiquity, convey an unlooked-for wisdom, that the gods, in the beginning, divided Man into men, that he might be more helpful to himself; just as the hand was divided into fingers, the better to answer its end.

The old fable covers a doctrine ever new and sublime; that there is One Man,—present to all particular men only partially, or through one faculty; and that you must take the whole society to find the whole man. Man is not a farmer, or a professor, or an engineer, but he is all. Man is priest, and scholar, and statesman, and producer, and soldier. In the divided or social state these functions are parceled out to individuals, each of whom aims to do his stint of the joint work, whilst each other performs his. The fable implies that the individual, to possess himself, must sometimes return from his own labor to embrace all the other laborers. But, unfortunately, this original unit, this fountain of power, has been so distributed to multitudes, has been so minutely subdivided and peddled out, that it is spilled into drops and cannot be gathered. The state of society is one in which the members have suffered amputation from the trunk, and strut about so many walking monsters—a good finger, a neck, a stomach, an elbow, but never a man.

Man is thus metamorphosed into a thing, into many things. The planter, who is Man sent out into the field to gather food, is seldom cheered by any idea of the true dignity of his ministry. He sees his bushel and his cart, and nothing beyond, and sinks into the farmer, instead of Man on the farm. The tradesman scarcely ever gives an ideal worth to his work, but is ridden by the routine of his craft, and the soul is subject to dollars. The priest becomes a form; the attorney, a statute book; the mechanic, a machine; the sailor, a rope of a ship.

In this distribution of functions the scholar is the delegated intellect. In the right state, he is Man Thinking. In the degenerate state, when the victim of society, he tends to become a mere thinker, or, still worse, the parrot of other men's thinking.

In this view of him, as Man Thinking, the theory of his office is contained. Him Nature solicits with all her placid, all her monitory pictures; him the past instructs; him the future invites. Is not, indeed, every man a student, and do not all things exist for the student's behoof? And, finally, is not the true scholar the only true master? But the old oracle said, "All things have two handles: beware of the wrong one." In life, too often the scholar errs with mankind and forfeits his privilege. Let us see him in his school, and consider him in reference to the main influences he receives.

The first in time and the first in importance of the influences upon the mind is that of Nature. Every day, the sun; and, after sunset, Night and her stars. Ever the winds blow; ever the grass grows. Every day, men and women, conversing, beholding and

beholden. The scholar is he of all men whom this spectacle most
engages. He must settle its value in his mind. What is Nature to
him? There is never a beginning, there is never an end, to the
inexplicable continuity of this web of God, but always circular
power returning into itself. Therein it resembles his own spirit,
whose beginning, whose ending, he never can find,—so entire,
so boundless. Far, too, as her splendors shine, system on system
shooting like rays upward, downward, without centre, without
circumference,—in the mass and in the particle, Nature hastens
to render account of herself to the mind. Classification begins.
To the young mind, everything is individual, stands by itself. By
and by it finds how to join two things, and see in them one
nature; then three, then three thousand; and so tyrannized over
by its own unifying instinct, it goes on tying things together,
diminishing anomalies, discovering roots running under ground,
whereby contrary and remote things cohere, and flower out from
one stem. It presently learns that since the dawn of history there
has been a constant accumulation and classifying of facts. But
what is classification but the perceiving that these objects are not
chaotic, and are not foreign, but have a law which is also a law
of the human mind? The astronomer discovers that geometry, a
pure abstraction of the human mind, is the measure of planetary
motion. The chemist finds proportions and intelligible method
throughout matter; and science is nothing but the finding of
analogy, identity, in the most remote parts. The ambitious soul
sits down before each refractory fact; one after another reduces
all strange constitutions, all new powers, to their class and their
law, and goes on forever to animate the last fibre of organization, the outskirts of nature, by insight.

Thus to him, to this school boy under the bending dome of
day, is suggested that he and it proceed from one root; one is leaf
and one is flower; relation, sympathy, stirring in every vein. And
what is that Root? Is not that the soul of his soul? A thought too
bold, a dream too wild. Yet when this spiritual light shall have

revealed the law of more earthly natures, when he has learned to worship the soul, and to see that the natural philosophy that now is, is only the first gropings of its gigantic hand, he shall look forward to an ever-expanding knowledge as to a becoming creator. He shall see that Nature is the opposite of the soul, answering to it part for part. One is seal and one is print. Its beauty is the beauty of his own mind. Its laws are the laws of his own mind. Nature then becomes to him the measure of his attainments. So much of Nature as he is ignorant of, so much of his own mind does he not yet possess. And, in fine, the ancient precept, "Know thyself," and the modern precept, "Study Nature," become at last one maxim.

The next great influence into the spirit of the scholar is the mind of the Past—in whatever form, whether of literature, of art, of institutions, that mind is inscribed. Books are the best type of the influence of the past. . . .

[T]he final value of action, like that of books, and better than books, is, that it is a resource. That great principle of Undulation in nature, that shows itself in the inspiring and expiring of the breath; in desire and satiety; in the ebb and flow of the sea; in day and night; in heat and cold; and as yet more deeply ingrained in every atom and every fluid, is known to us under the name of Polarity,—these "fits of easy transmission and reflection," as Newton called them, are the law of Nature because they are the law of spirit.

The mind now thinks, now acts; and each fit reproduces the other. When the artist has exhausted his materials, when the fancy no longer paints, when thoughts are no longer apprehended, and books are a weariness,—he has always the resource to live. Character is higher than intellect. Thinking is the function. Living is the functionary. The stream retreats to its source. A great soul will be strong to live, as well as strong to think. Does he lack organ or medium to impart his truths? He can still fall back on this elemental force of living them. This is a total act. Thinking is a partial act. Let the grandeur of justice shine in his affairs. Let the beauty of affection cheer his lowly roof. Those "far from fame," who dwell and act with him, will feel the force of his constitution in the doings and passages of the day better than it can be measured by any public and designed display. Time shall teach him that the scholar loses no hour which the man lives. Herein he unfolds the sacred germ of his instinct, screened from influence. What is lost in seemliness is gained in strength. Not out of those, on whom systems of education have exhausted their culture, comes the helpful giant to destroy the old or to build the new, but out of unhandselled savage nature, out of terrible Druids and berserkirs, come at last Alfred and Shakespeare.

I hear, therefore, with joy whatever is beginning to be said of the dignity and necessity of labor to every citizen. There is virtue yet in the hoe and the spade, for learned as well as for unlearned hands. And labor is everywhere welcome; always we are invited to work; only be this limitation observed, that a man shall not for the sake of wider activity sacrifice any opinion to the popular judgments and modes of action.

I have now spoken of the education of the scholar by Nature, by books, and by action. It remains to say somewhat of his duties.

They are such as become Man Thinking. They may all be comprised in self-trust. The office of the scholar is to cheer, to raise, and to guide men by showing them facts amidst appearances. He plies the slow, unhonored, and unpaid task of observation. Flamsteed and Herschel, in their glazed observatories, may catalogue the stars with the praise of all men, and, the results being splendid and useful, honor is sure. But he, in his private observatory, cataloguing obscure and nebulous stars of the human mind, which as yet no man has thought of as such,—watching days and months, sometimes, for a few facts; correcting still his old records,—must relinquish display and immediate fame.

In the long period of his preparation he must betray often an
ignorance and shiftlessness in popular arts, incurring the disdain
of the able, who shoulder him aside. Long he must stammer in
his speech; often forego the living for the dead. Worse yet, he
must accept—how often!—poverty and solitude. For the ease
and pleasure of treading the old road, accepting the fashions, the
education, the religion of society, he takes the cross of making
his own, and, of course, the self-accusation, the faint heart, the
frequent uncertainty and loss of time, which are the nettles and
tangling vines in the way of the self-relying and self-directed;
and the state of virtual hostility in which he seems to stand to
society, and especially to educated society. For all this loss and
scorn, what offset? He is to find consolation in exercising the
highest functions of human nature. He is one who raises himself
from private considerations, and breathes and lives on public
and illustrious thoughts. He is the world's eye. He is the world's
heart. He is to resist the vulgar prosperity that retrogrades ever
to barbarism, by preserving and communicating heroic sentiments, noble biographies, melodious verse, and the conclusions
of history. Whatsoever oracles the human heart, in all emergen-
cies, in all solemn hours, has uttered as its commentary on the
world of actions,—these he shall receive and impart. And whatsoever new verdict Reason from her inviolable seat pronounces
on the passing men and events of today,—this he shall hear and
promulgate.

These being his functions, it becomes him to feel all confidence in himself, and to defer never to the popular cry. He and
he only knows the world. The world of any moment is the mer-
est appearance. Some great decorum, some fetish of a government, some ephemeral trade, or war, or man, is cried up by half
mankind and cried down by the other half, as if all depended on
this particular up or down. The odds are that the whole question
is not worth the poorest thought which the scholar has lost in
listening to the controversy. Let him not quit his belief that a

popgun is a popgun, though the ancient and honorable of the earth affirm it to be the crack of doom. In silence, in steadiness, in severe abstraction, let him hold by himself; add observation to observation, patient of neglect, patient of reproach; and bide his own time,—happy enough if he can satisfy himself alone, that this day he has seen something truly. Success treads on every right step. For the instinct is sure that prompts him to tell his brother what he thinks. He then learns that in going down into the secrets of his own mind he has descended into the secrets of all minds. He learns that he who has mastered any law in his private thoughts is master to that extent of all men whose language he speaks, and of all into whose language his own can be translated. The poet, in utter solitude remembering his spontaneous thoughts and recording them, is found to have recorded that which men in crowded cities find true for them also. The orator distrusts at first the fitness of his frank confessions,—his want of knowledge of the persons he addresses,—until he finds that he is the complement of his hearers; that they drink his words because he fulfils for them their own nature; the deeper he dives into his privatest, secretest presentiment, to his wonder he finds this is the most acceptable, most public, and universally true. The people delight in it; the better part of every man feels, This is my music; this is myself.

In self-trust all the virtues are comprehended. Free should the scholar be,—free and brave. Free even to the definition of freedom, "without any hindrance that does not arise out of his own constitution." Brave; for fear is a thing which a scholar by his very function puts behind him. Fear always springs from ignorance. It is a shame to him if his tranquility, amid dangerous times, arise from the presumption that, like children and women, his is a protected class; or if he seek a temporary peace by the diversion of his thoughts from politics or vexed questions, hiding his head like an ostrich in the flowering bushes, peeping into microscopes, and turning rhymes, as a boy whistles to keep his courage up. So is the danger a danger still; so is the fear worse. Manlike let him turn and face it. Let him look into its eye and search its nature, inspect its origin,—see the whelping of this lion, which lies no great way back; he will then find in himself a perfect comprehension of its nature and extent; he will have made his hands meet on the other side, and can henceforth defy it, and pass on superior. The world is his, who can see through its pretension. What deafness, what stone-blind custom, what overgrown error you behold, is there only by sufferance,—by your sufferance. See it to be a lie, and you have already dealt it its mortal blow.

Yes, we are the cowed—we the trustless. It is a mischievous notion that we are come late into Nature; that the world was finished a long time ago. As the world was plastic and fluid in the hands of God, so it is ever to so much of his attributes as we bring to it. To ignorance and sin, it is flint. They adapt them-selves to it as they may; but in proportion as a man has any-thing in him divine, the firmament flows before him and takes his signet and form. Not he is great who can alter matter, but he who can alter my state of mind. They are the kings of the world who give the color of their present thought to all nature and all art, and persuade men by the cheerful serenity of their carrying the matter, that this thing which they do is the apple which the ages have desired to pluck, now at last ripe, and inviting nations to the harvest. The great man makes the great thing. Wherever Macdonald sits, there is the head of the table. Linnaeus makes botany the most alluring of studies, and wins it from the farmer and the herb-woman; Davy, chemistry; and Cuvier, fossils. The day is always his, who works in it with serenity and great aims. The unstable estimates of men crowd to him whose mind is filled with a truth, as the heaped waves of the Atlantic follow the moon.

For this self-trust, the reason is deeper than can be fathomed, darker than can be enlightened. I might not carry with me the feeling of my audience in stating my own belief. But I have already shown the ground of my hope, in adverting to the doctrine that man is one. I believe man has been wronged; he has wronged himself. He has almost lost the light that can lead him back to his prerogatives. Men are become of no account. Men in history, men in the world of to-day are bugs, are spawn, and are called "the mass" and "the herd." In a century, in a millennium, one or two men; that is to say, one or two approximations to the right state of every man. All the rest behold in the hero or the poet their own green and crude being,—ripened; yes, and are content to be less, so that may attain to its full stature. What a testimony, full of grandeur, full of pity, is borne to the demands of his own nature by the poor clansman, the poor partisan, who rejoices in the glory of his chief. The poor and the low find some amends to their immense moral capacity for their acquiescence in a political and social inferiority. They are content to be brushed like flies from the path of a great person, so that justice shall be done by him to that common nature which it is the dearest desire of all to see enlarged and glorified. They sun themselves in the great man's light, and feel it to be their own element. They cast the dignity of man from their downtrod selves upon the shoulders of a hero, and will perish to add one drop of blood to make that great heart beat, those giant sinews combat and conquer. He lives for us, and we live in him.

Men such as they are, very naturally seek money or power; and power because it is as good as money,—the "spoils," so called, "of office." And why not? for they aspire to the highest, and this, in their sleep-walking, they dream is highest. Wake them, and they shall quit the false good, and leap to the true, and leave governments to clerks and desks. This revolution is to be wrought by the gradual domestication of the idea of Culture. The main enterprise of the world for splendor, for extent, is the upbuilding of a man. Here are the materials strewn along the ground. The private life of one man shall be a more illustrious monarchy,—more formidable to its enemy, more sweet and serene in its influence to its friend, than any kingdom in history. For a man, rightly viewed, comprehendeth the particular natures of all men. Each philosopher, each bard, each actor, has only done for me, as by a delegate, what one day I can do for myself. The books which once we valued more than the apple of the eye we have quite exhausted. What is that but saying that we have come up with the point of view which the universal mind took through the eyes of one scribe; we have been that man, and have passed on. First one, then another, we drain all cisterns, and, waxing greater by all these supplies, we crave a better and more abundant food. The man has never lived that can feed us ever. The human mind cannot be enshrined in a person who shall set a barrier on any one side to this unbounded, unboundable empire. It is one central fire, which, flaming now out of the lips of Etna, lightens the capes of Sicily; and now out of the throat of Vesuvius, illuminates the towers and vineyards of Naples. It is one light which beams out of a thousand stars. It is one soul which animates all men.

But I have dwelt perhaps tediously upon this abstraction of the Scholar. I ought not to delay longer to add what I have to say of nearer reference to the time and to this country.

Historically there is thought to be a difference in the ideas which predominate over successive epochs, and there are data for marking the genius of the Classic, of the Romantic, and now of the Reflective or Philosophical age. With the views I have intimated of the oneness or the identity of the mind through all individuals, I do not much dwell on these differences. In fact, I believe each individual passes through all three. The boy is a Greek; the youth, romantic; the adult, reflective. I deny not, however, that a revolution in the leading idea may be distinctly enough traced.

Our age is bewailed as the age of Introversion. Must that needs be evil? We, it seems, are critical; we are embarrassed with second thoughts; we cannot enjoy anything for hankering to know whereof the pleasure consists; we are lined with eyes; we see with our feet the time is infected with Hamlet's unhappiness,—"Sicklied o'er with the pale cast of thought."

Is it so bad then? Sight is the last thing to be pitied. Would we be blind? Do we fear lest we should outsee Nature and God, and drink truth dry? I look upon the discontent of the literary class as a mere announcement of the fact that they find themselves not in the state of mind of their fathers, and regret the coming state as untried; as a boy dreads the water before he has learned that he can swim. If there is any period one would desire to be born in, is it not the age of Revolution; when the old and the new stand side by side, and admit of being compared; when the energies of all men are searched by fear and by hope; when the historic glories of the old can be compensated by the rich possibilities of the new era? This time, like all times, is a very good one, if we but know what to do with it.

I read with joy of the auspicious signs of the coming days, as they glimmer already through poetry and art, through philosophy and science, through church and state.

One of these signs is the fact that the same movement which affected the elevation of what was called the lowest class in the state, assumed in literature a very marked and as benign an aspect. Instead of the sublime and beautiful; the near, the low, the common, was explored and poetized. That which had been negligently trodden under foot by those who were harnessing and provisioning themselves for long journeys into far countries, is suddenly found to be richer than all foreign parts. The literature of the poor, the feelings of the child, the philosophy of the street, the meaning of household life, are the topics of the time. It is a great stride. It is a sign—is it not?—of new vigor, when the extremities are made active, when currents of warm life run into the hands and feet. I ask not for the great, the remote, the romantic; what is doing in Italy or Arabia; what is Greek art or

Provençal minstrelsy; I embrace the common, I explore and sit at the feet of the familiar, the low. Give me insight into today, and you may have the antique and future worlds. What would we really know the meaning of? The meal in the firkin, the milk in the pan, the ballad in the street, the news of the boat, the glance of the eye, the form and the gait of the body,—show me the ultimate reason of these matters; show me the sublime presence of the highest spiritual cause lurking, as always it does lurk, in these suburbs and extremities of nature; let me see every trifle bristling with the polarity that ranges it instantly on an eternal law; and the shop, the plough, and the ledger, referred to the like cause by which light undulates and poets sing;—and the world lies no longer a dull miscellany and lumber-room, but has form and order; there is no trifle, there is no puzzle, but one design unites and animates the farthest pinnacle and the lowest trench.

This idea has inspired the genius of Goldsmith, Burns, Cowper, and, in a newer time, of Goethe, Wordsworth, and Carlyle. This idea they have differently followed and with various success. In contrast with their writing, the style of Pope, of Johnson, of Gibbon, looks cold and pedantic. This writing is blood-warm. Man is surprised to find that things near are not less beautiful and wondrous than things remote. The near explains the far. The drop is a small ocean. A man is related to all nature. This perception of the worth of the vulgar is fruitful in discoveries. Goethe, in this very thing the most modern of the moderns, has shown us, as none ever did, the genius of the ancients.

There is one man of genius who has done much for this philosophy of life, whose literary value has never yet been rightly estimated; I mean Emanuel Swedenborg. The most imaginative of men, yet writing with the precision of a mathematician, he endeavored to engraft a purely philosophical Ethics on the popular Christianity of his time. Such an attempt, of course, must have difficulty which no genius could surmount. But he saw and showed the connection between nature and the affections of the soul. He pierced the emblematic or spiritual character of the visible, audible, tangible world. Especially did his shade-loving muse hover over and interpret the lower parts of nature; he showed the mysterious bond that allies moral evil to the foul material forms, and has given in epical parables a theory of insanity, of beasts, of unclean and fearful things.

Another sign of our times, also marked by an analogous political movement, is the new importance given to the single person. Everything that tends to insulate the individual—to surround him with barriers of natural respect, so that each man shall feel the world is his and man shall treat with man as a sovereign state with a sovereign state—tends to true union as well as greatness. "I learned," said the melancholy Pestalozzi, "that no man in God's wide earth is either willing or able to help any other man." Help must come from the bosom alone. The scholar is that man who must take up into himself all the ability of the time, all the contributions of the past, all the hopes of the future. He must be a university of knowledges. If there be one lesson more than another which should pierce his ear, it is, The world is nothing, the man is all; in yourself is the law of all nature, and you know not yet how a globule of sap ascends; in yourself slumbers the whole of Reason; it is for you to know all, it is for you to dare all. Mr. President and Gentlemen, this confidence in the unsearched might of man belongs, by all motives, by all prophecy, by all preparation, to the American Scholar. We have listened too long to the courtly muses of Europe. The spirit of the American freeman is already suspected to be timid, imitative, tame. Public and private avarice make the air we breathe thick and fat. The scholar is decent, indolent, complaisant. See already the tragic consequence. The mind of this country, taught to aim at low objects, eats upon itself. There is no work for any but the decorous and the complaisant. Young men of the fairest promise, who begin life upon our shores, inflated by the mountain winds, shined upon by all the stars of God, find the earth below not in unison with these, but are hindered from action by the disgust which the principles on which business is managed inspire, and turn drudges or die of disgust—some of them suicides. What is the remedy? They did not yet see, and thousands of young men as hopeful now crowding to the barriers for the career do not yet see, that if the single man plant himself indomitably on his instincts, and there abide, the huge world will come round to him. Patience, patience; with the shades of all the good and great for company; and for solace, the perspective of your own infinite life; and for work, the study and the communication of principles, the making those instincts prevalent, the conversion of the world. Is it not the chief disgrace in the world not to be a unit, not to be reckoned one character, not to yield that peculiar fruit; which each man was created to bear; but to be reckoned in the gross, in the hundred, or the thousand, of the party, the section, to which we belong; and our opinion predicted geographically, as the north, or the south? Not so, brothers and friends,—please God, ours shall not be so. We will walk on our own feet; we will work with our own hands; we will speak our own minds. The study of letters shall be no longer a name for pity, for doubt, and for sensual indulgence. The dread of man and the love of man shall be a wall of defence and a wreath of joy around all. A nation of men will for the first time exist, because each believes himself inspired by the Divine Soul which also inspires all men.

"EXPOSITORS OF THE DIVINE MIND"

Taken from his manifesto, Nature, *here RWE articulates, more successfully than in other places, his approach to Spirit, which is similar to a view of the world as God-embodied, personal, accessible, and subtle.*

Of that ineffable essence which we call Spirit, he that thinks most, will say least. We can foresee God in the coarse, and, as it were, distant phenomena of matter; but when we try to define and describe himself, both language and thought desert us, and we are as helpless as fools and savages. That essence refuses to be recorded in propositions, but when man has worshipped him intellectually, the noblest ministry of nature is to stand as the apparition of God. It is the organ through which the universal spirit speaks to the individual, and strives to lead back the individual to it.

When we consider Spirit, we see that the views already presented do not include the whole circumference of man. We must add some related thoughts.

Three problems are put by nature to the mind; What is matter? Whence is it? and Whereto? The first of these questions only, the ideal theory answers. Idealism saith: matter is a phenomenon, not a substance. Idealism acquaints us with the total disparity between the evidence of our own being, and the evidence of the world's being. The one is perfect; the other, incapable of any assurance; the mind is a part of the nature of things; the world is a divine dream, from which we may presently awake to the glories and certainties of day. Idealism is a hypothesis to account for nature by other principles than those of carpentry and chemistry. Yet, if it only deny the existence of matter, it does not satisfy the demands of the spirit. It leaves God out of me. It leaves me in the splendid labyrinth of my perceptions, to wander without end. Then the heart resists it, because it balks the affections in denying substantive being to men and women. Nature is so pervaded with human life, that there is something of humanity in all, and in every particular. But this theory makes nature foreign to me, and does not account for that consanguinity which we acknowledge to it.

Let it stand, then, in the present state of our knowledge, merely as a useful introductory hypothesis, serving to apprize us of the eternal distinction between the soul and the world.

But when, following the invisible steps of thought, we come to inquire, Whence is matter? and Whereto? many truths arise to us out of the recesses of consciousness. We learn that the highest is present to the soul of man, that the dread universal essence, which is not wisdom, or love, or beauty, or power, but all in one, and each entirely, is that for which all things exist, and that by which they are; that spirit creates; that behind nature, throughout nature, spirit is present; one and not compound, it does not act upon us from without, that is, in space and time, but spiritually, or through ourselves: therefore, that spirit, that is, the Supreme Being, does not build up nature around us, but puts it forth through us, as the life of the tree puts forth new branches and leaves through the pores of the old. As a plant upon the earth, so a man rests upon the bosom of God; he is nourished by unfailing fountains, and draws, at his need, inexhaustible power. Who can set bounds to the possibilities of man? Once inhale the upper air, being admitted to behold the absolute natures of justice and truth, and we learn that man has access to the entire mind of the Creator, is himself the creator in the finite. This view, which admonishes me where the sources of wisdom and power lie, and points to virtue as to

> "The golden key
> Which opes the palace of eternity,"

carries upon its face the highest certificate of truth, because it animates me to create my own world through the purification of my soul.

The world proceeds from the same spirit as the body of man. It is a remoter and inferior incarnation of God, a projection of God in the unconscious. But it differs from the body in one important respect. It is not, like that, now subjected to the human will. Its serene order is inviolable by us. It is, therefore, to us, the present expositor of the divine mind. It is a fixed point whereby we may measure our departure. As we degenerate, the contrast between us and our house is more evident. We are as much strangers in nature, as we are aliens from God. We do not understand the notes of birds. The fox and the deer run away from us; the bear and tiger rend us. We do not know the uses of more than a few plants, as corn and the apple, the potato and the vine. Is not the landscape, every glimpse of which hath a grandeur, a face of him? Yet this may show us what discord is between man and nature, for you cannot freely admire a noble landscape, if laborers are digging in the field hard by. The poet finds something ridiculous in his delight, until he is out of the sight of men.

"WITHIN MAN IS THE SOUL OF THE WHOLE"

From the famously philosophical, somewhat obscurely mystical essay, "The Over-Soul," this passage, as clearly as any, attempts to explain his mature metaphysics.

There is a difference between one and another hour of life, in their authority and subsequent effect. Our faith comes in moments; our vice is habitual. Yet there is a depth in those brief moments which constrains us to ascribe more reality to them than to all other experiences. For this reason, the argument which is always forthcoming to silence those who conceive extraordinary hopes of man, namely, the appeal to experience, is for ever invalid and vain. We give up the past to the objector, and yet we hope. He must explain this hope. We grant that human life is mean; but how did we find out that it was mean? What is the ground of this uneasiness of ours; of this old discontent? What is the universal sense of want and ignorance, but the fine innuendo by which the soul makes its enormous claim? Why do men feel that the natural history of man has never been written, but he is always leaving behind what you have said of him, and it becomes old, and books of metaphysics worthless? The philosophy of six thousand years has not searched the chambers and magazines of the soul. In its experiments there has always remained, in the last analysis, a residuum it could not resolve. Man is a stream whose source is hidden. Our being is descending into us from we know not whence. The most exact calculator has no prescience that somewhat incalculable may not balk the very next moment. I am constrained every moment to acknowledge a higher origin for events than the will I call mine.

As with events, so is it with thoughts. When I watch that flowing river, which, out of regions I see not, pours for a season its streams into me, I see that I am a pensioner; not a cause, but a surprised spectator of this ethereal water; that I desire and look up, and put myself in the attitude of reception, but from some alien energy the visions come.

The Supreme Critic on the errors of the past and the present, and the only prophet of that which must be, is that great nature in which we rest, as the earth lies in the soft arms of the atmosphere; that Unity, that Over-soul, within which every man's particular being is contained and made one with all other; that common heart, of which all sincere conversation is the worship, to which all right action is submission; that overpowering reality which confutes our tricks and talents, and constrains every one to pass for what he is, and to speak from his character, and not from his tongue, and which evermore tends to pass into our thought and hand, and become wisdom, and virtue, and power, and beauty. We live in succession, in division, in parts, in particles. Meantime within man is the soul of the whole; the wise silence; the universal beauty, to which every part and particle is equally related; the eternal ONE.

2

"We Must Be Lovers" (Divinity and the Soul)

The phrase that gives the name to this chapter could just as easily have come from the first sentence in the first selection, below: "the Highest dwells with him"—a powerful conclusion to RWE's metaphysical essay explaining his mature belief in the nature, quality, and location of the Divine. All of the selections in this chapter reflect RWE's abiding understanding of God as available, inspiring, spirit, indwelling, and elusive—and the duties each person enjoys and discovers innately by knowing the Divine in these ways.

"THE SURGES OF EVERLASTING NATURE ENTER INTO ME"

These are the final two, long paragraphs from "The Over-Soul," Essays: First.

Let man, then, learn the revelation of all nature and all thought to his heart; this, namely; that the Highest dwells with him; that the sources of nature are in his own mind, if the sentiment of duty is there. But if he would know what the great God speaketh, he must "go into his closet and shut the door," as Jesus said. God will not make himself manifest to cowards. He must greatly listen to himself, withdrawing himself from all the accents of other men's devotion. Even their prayers are hurtful to him, until he have made his own. Our religion vulgarly stands on numbers of believers. Whenever the appeal is made—no matter how indirectly—to numbers, proclamation is then and there made, that religion is not. He that finds God a sweet, enveloping thought to him never counts his company. When I sit in that presence, who shall dare to come in? When I rest in perfect humility, when I burn with pure love, what can Calvin or Swedenborg say?

It makes no difference whether the appeal is to numbers or to one. The faith that stands on authority is not faith. The reliance on authority measures the decline of religion, the withdrawal of the soul. The position men have given to Jesus, now for many centuries of history, is a position of authority. It characterizes themselves. It cannot alter the eternal facts. Great is the soul, and plain. It is no flatterer, it is no follower; it never appeals from itself. It believes in itself. Before the immense possibilities of man, all mere experience, all past biography, however spotless and sainted, shrinks away. Before that heaven which our presentiments foreshow us, we cannot easily praise any form of life we have seen or read of. We not only affirm that we have few great men, but, absolutely speaking, that we have none; that we have no history, no record of any character or mode of living, that entirely contents us. The saints and demigods whom history worships we are constrained to accept with a grain of allowance. Though in our lonely hours we draw a new strength out of their memory, yet, pressed on our attention, as they are by the thoughtless and customary, they fatigue and invade. The soul gives itself, alone, original, and pure, to the Lonely, Original, and Pure, who, on that condition, gladly inhabits, leads, and speaks through it. Then is it glad, young, and nimble. It is not wise, but it sees through all things. It is not called religious, but it is innocent. It calls the light its own, and feels that the grass grows and the stone falls by a law inferior to, and dependent on, its nature. Behold, it saith, I am born into the great, the universal mind. I, the imperfect, adore my own Perfect. I am somehow receptive of the great soul, and thereby I do overlook the sun and the stars, and feel them to be the fair accidents and effects which change and pass. More and more the surges of everlasting nature enter into me, and I become public and human in my regards and actions. So come I to live in thoughts, and act with energies, which are immortal. Thus revering the soul, and learning, as the ancient said, that "its beauty is immense," man will come to see that the world is the perennial miracle which the soul worketh, and be less astonished at particular wonders; he will learn that there is no profane history; that all history is sacred; that the universe is represented in an atom, in a moment of time. He will weave no longer a spotted life of shreds and patches, but he will live with a divine unity. He will cease from what is base and frivolous in his life, and be content with all places and with any service he can render. He will calmly front the morrow in the negligency of that trust which carries God with it, and so hath already the whole future in the bottom of the heart.

"WE MUST BE LOVERS"

In one enormous, breathless, paragraph RWE urges his audience to find ways to love one another that resemble the best of what Christianity has demonstrated in the past, and yet, surpass it. This is taken from the essay, "Man the Reformer."

We must be lovers, and at once the impossible becomes possible. Our age and history, for these thousand years, has not been the history of kindness, but of selfishness. Our distrust is very expensive. The money we spend for courts and prisons is very ill laid out. We make, by distrust, the thief, and burglar, and incendiary, and by our court and jail we keep him so. An acceptance of the sentiment of love throughout Christendom for a season, would bring the felon and the outcast to our side in tears, with the devotion of his faculties to our service. See this wide society of laboring men and women. We allow ourselves to be served by them, we live apart from them, and meet them without a salute in the streets. We do not greet their talents, nor rejoice in their good fortune, nor foster their hopes, nor in the assembly of the people vote for what is dear to them. Thus we enact the part of the selfish noble and king from the foundation of the world. See, this tree always bears one fruit. In every household, the peace of a pair is poisoned by the malice, slyness, indolence, and alienation of domestics. Let any two matrons meet, and observe how soon their conversation turns on the troubles from their "help," as our phrase is. In every knot of laborers, the rich man does not feel himself among his friends,—and at the polls he finds them arrayed in a mass in distinct opposition to him. We complain that the politics of masses of the people are controlled by designing men, and led in opposition to manifest justice and the common weal, and to their own interest. But the people do not wish to be represented or ruled by the ignorant and base. They only vote for these, because they were asked with the voice and semblance of kindness. They will not vote for them long. They inevitably prefer wit and probity. To use an Egyptian metaphor, it is not their will for any long time "to raise the nails of wild beasts, and to depress the heads of the sacred birds." Let our affection flow out to our fellows; it would operate in a day the greatest of all revolutions. It is better to work on institutions by the sun than by the wind. The state must consider the poor man, and all voices must speak for him. Every child that is born must have a just chance for his bread. Let the amelioration in our laws of property proceed from the concession of the rich, not from the grasping of the poor. Let us begin by habitual imparting. Let us understand that the equitable rule is, that no one should take more than his share, let him be ever so rich. Let me feel that I am to be a lover. I am to see to it that the world is the better for me, and to find my reward in the act. Love would put a new face on this weary old world in which we dwell as pagans and enemies too long, and it would warm the heart to see how fast the vain diplomacy of statesmen, the impotence of armies, and navies, and lines of defence, would be superseded by this unarmed child. Love will creep where it cannot go, will accomplish that by imperceptible methods,—being its own lever, fulcrum, and power,—which force could never achieve. Have you not seen in the woods, in a late autumn morning, a poor fungus or mushroom,—a plant without any solidity, nay, that seemed nothing but a soft mush or jelly,—by its constant, total, and inconceivably gentle pushing, manage to break its way up through the frosty ground, and actually to lift a hard crust on its head? It is the symbol of the power of kindness. The virtue of this principle in human society in application to great interests is obsolete and forgotten. Once or twice in history it has been tried in illustrious instances, with signal success. This great, overgrown, dead Christendom of ours still keeps alive at least the name of a lover of mankind. But one day all men will be lovers; and every calamity will be dissolved in the universal sunshine.

"EACH INDIVIDUAL SOUL"

A portion of another single long paragraph, this time from an 1841 lecture, "The Method of Nature," this passage begins to reveal how complex and subtle was RWE's understanding of nature—surely more spiritually subtle than what we might today call the "natural world."

The universal does not attract us until housed in an individual. Who heeds the waste abyss of possibility? The ocean is everywhere the same, but it has no character until seen with the shore or the ship. Who would value any number of miles of Atlantic brine bounded by lines of latitude and longitude? Confine it by granite rocks, let it wash a shore where wise men dwell, and it is filled with expression; and the point of greatest interest is where the land and water meet. So must we admire in man, the form of the formless, the concentration of the vast, the house of reason, the cave of memory. See the play of thoughts! What nimble gigantic creatures are these! What saurians, what palaiotheria shall be named with these agile movers? The great Pan of old, who was clothed in a leopard skin to signify the beautiful variety of things, and the firmament, his coat of stars,—was but the representative of thee, O rich and various Man! Thou palace of sight and sound, carrying in thy senses the morning and the night and the unfathomable galaxy; in thy brain, the geometry of the City of God; in thy heart, the bower of love and the realms of right and wrong. An individual man is a fruit which it cost all the foregoing ages to form and ripen. The history of the genesis or the old mythology repeats itself in the experience of every child. He too is a demon or god thrown into a particular chaos, where he strives ever to lead things from disorder into order. Each individual soul is such, in virtue of its being a power to translate the world into some particular language of its own; if not into a picture, a statue, or a dance,—why, then, into a trade, an art, a science, a mode of living, a conversation, a character, an influence.

REPLACING SIN WITH DISCOVERY

RWE is everywhere and always self-consciously post-Christian. Here, from "The Method of Nature," he lays out his vision for a new kind of worship, perception, and discovery, still building on the spirit and work of the first Christians who settled the American territories.

What is all history but the work of ideas, a record of the incomputable energy which his infinite aspirations infuse into man? Has any thing grand and lasting been done? Who did it? Plainly not any man, but all men: it was the prevalence and inundation of an idea. What brought the pilgrims here? One man says, civil liberty; another, the desire of founding a church; and a third, discovers that the motive force was plantation and trade. But if the

Puritans could rise from the dust, they could not answer. It is to be seen in what they were, and not in what they designed; it was the growth and expansion of the human race, and resembled herein the sequent Revolution, which was not begun in Concord, or Lexington, or Virginia, but was the overflowing of the sense of natural right in every clear and active spirit of the period. Is a man boastful and knowing, and his own master?—we turn from him without hope: but let him be filled with awe and dread before the Vast and the Divine, which uses him glad to be used, and our eye is riveted to the chain of events. What a debt is ours to that old religion which, in the childhood of most of us, still dwelt like a sabbath morning in the country of New England, teaching privation, self-denial and sorrow! A man was born not for prosperity, but to suffer for the benefit of others, like the noble rock maple which all around our villages bleeds for the service of man. Not praise, not men's acceptance of our doing, but the spirit's holy errand through us absorbed the thought. How dignified was this! How all that is called talents and success, in our noisy capitals, becomes buzz and din before this man-worthiness! How our friendships and the complaisances we use, shame us now! Shall we not quit our companions, as if they were thieves and pot-companions, and betake ourselves to some desert cliff of mount Katahdin, some unvisited recess in Moosehead Lake, to bewail our innocency and to recover it, and with it the power to communicate again with these sharers of a more sacred idea?

And what is to replace for us the piety of that race? We cannot have theirs: it glides away from us day by day, but we also can bask in the great morning which rises forever out of the eastern sea, and be ourselves the children of the light. I stand here to say, Let us worship the mighty and transcendent Soul. It is the office, I doubt not, of this age to annul that adulterous divorce which the superstition of many ages has effected between the intellect and holiness. The lovers of goodness have been one class, the students of wisdom another, as if either could exist in any purity without the other. Truth is always holy, holiness always wise. I will that we keep terms with sin, and a sinful literature and society, no longer, but live a life of discovery and performance. Accept the intellect, and it will accept us. Be the lowly ministers of that pure omniscience, and deny it not before men. It will burn up all profane literature, all base current opinions, all the false powers of the world, as in a moment of time. I draw from nature the lesson of an intimate divinity. Our health and reason as men needs our respect to this fact, against the heedlessness and against the contradiction of society. The sanity of man needs the poise of this immanent force. His nobility needs the assurance of this inexhaustible reserved power. How great soever have been its bounties, they are a drop to the sea whence they flow. If you say, "the acceptance of the vision is also the act of God:"—I shall not seek to penetrate the mystery, I admit the force of what you say. If you ask, "How can any rules be given for the attainment of gifts so sublime?" I shall only remark that the solicitations of this spirit, as long as there is life, are never forborne. Tenderly, tenderly, they woo and court us from every object in nature, from every fact in life, from every thought in the mind. The one condition coupled with the gift of truth is its use. That man shall be learned who reduceth his learning to practice. Emanuel Swedenborg affirmed that it was opened to him, "that the spirits who knew truth in this life, but did it not, at death shall lose their knowledge." "If knowledge," said Ali the Caliph, "calleth unto practice, well; if not, it goeth away." The only way into nature is to enact our best insight. Instantly we are higher poets, and can speak a deeper law. Do what you know, and perception is converted into character, as islands and continents were built by invisible infusories, or, as these forest leaves absorb light, electricity, and volatile gases, and the gnarled oak to live a thousand years is the arrest and fixation of the most volatile and ethereal currents. The doctrine of this Supreme

Presence is a cry of joy and exultation. Who shall dare think he has come late into nature, or has missed anything excellent in the past, who seeth the admirable stars of possibility, and the yet untouched continent of hope glittering with all its mountains in the vast West? I praise with wonder this great reality, which seems to drown all things in the deluge of its light. What man seeing this, can lose it from his thoughts, or entertain a meaner subject? The entrance of this into his mind seems to be the birth of man. We cannot describe the natural history of the soul, but we know that it is divine. I cannot tell if these wonderful qualities which house to-day in this mortal frame, shall ever reassemble in equal activity in a similar frame, or whether they have before had a natural history like that of this body you see before you; but this one thing I know, that these qualities did not now begin to exist, cannot be sick with my sickness, nor buried in any grave; but that they circulate through the Universe: before the world was, they were. Nothing can bar them out, or shut them in, but they penetrate the ocean and land, space and time, form and essence, and hold the key to universal nature. I draw from this faith courage and hope. All things are known to the soul. It is not to be surprised by any communication. Nothing can be greater than it. Let those fear and those fawn who will. The soul is in her native realm, and it is wider than space, older than time, wide as hope, rich as love. Pusillanimity and fear she refuses with a beautiful scorn: they are not for her who putteth on her coronation robes, and goes out through universal love to universal power.

"THAT SHUDDER OF AWE AND DELIGHT"

Taken from his philosophical, mystical essay of metaphysics, "The Over-Soul," Essays: First, *this single long paragraph speaks most directly to RWE's belief—carried out in many practical expressions in his own life, and, for instance, in the peripatetics of his student, Thoreau—in how divine revelation works.*

We distinguish the announcements of the soul, its manifestations of its own nature, by the term "Revelation." These are always attended by the emotion of the sublime. For this communication is an influx of the Divine mind into our mind. It is an ebb of the individual rivulet before the flowing surges of the sea of life. Every distinct apprehension of this central commandment agitates men with awe and delight. A thrill passes through all men at the reception of new truth, or at the performance of a great action, which comes out of the heart of nature. In these communications, the power to see is not separated from the will to do, but the insight proceeds from obedience, and the obedience proceeds from a joyful perception. Every moment when the individual feels himself invaded by it is memorable. By the necessity of our constitution, a certain enthusiasm attends the individual's consciousness of that divine presence. The character and duration of this enthusiasm varies with the state of the individual, from an ecstasy and trance and prophetic inspiration,—which is its rarer appearance,—to the faintest glow of virtuous emotion, in which form it warms, like our household fires, all the families and associations of men, and makes society possible. A certain tendency to insanity has always attended the opening of the religious sense in men, as if they had been "blasted with excess of light." The trances of Socrates, the "union" of Plotinus, the vision of Porphyry, the conversion of Paul, the aurora of Behmen, the convulsions of George Fox and his Quakers, the illumination of Swedenborg, are of this kind. What was in the case of these remarkable persons a ravishment has, in innumerable instances in common life, been exhibited in less striking manner. Everywhere the history of religion betrays a tendency to enthusiasm. The rapture of the Moravian and Quietist; the opening of the internal sense of the Word, in the language of the New Jerusalem Church; the *revival* of the Calvinistic churches; the *experiences* of the Methodists, are varying forms of that shudder of awe and delight with which the individual soul always mingles with the universal soul.

TRANSLATIONS OF HAFIZ

RWE began his exploration of the religious traditions of the East at about the same time that his Christian ministry began to disintegrate. It is difficult to say whether the one led to the other; certainly, they were of the same questing spirit. Regardless, the Hafiz that RWE discovered with the translations he published in a single issue of Atlantic Monthly, *April 1858, show remarkable similarities to the RWE that had by then emerged fully into view. It is RWE who brought the Persian Sufi poet into the American consciousness. His translations of Hafiz may not be entirely faithful to the Persian originals, but there were no accessible originals to be had, and scholarship hadn't yet created any sort of standard edition of the works in the original. In our own day, the poet Daniel Ladinsky has created bestselling volumes of Hafiz by doing precisely what RWE did more than a century before: paraphrasing the language, thereby translating "the spirit" of the poems.*

The Wheel of Heaven

I batter the wheel of heaven
When it rolls not rightly by;
I am not one of the snivellers
Who fall thereon and die.

Roses Burn

See how the roses burn!
Bring wine to quench the fire!
Alas! The flames come up with us,—
We perish with desire.

Wine and Wonder

The Builder of heaven
Hath sundered the earth,
So that no footway
Leads out of it forth.

On turnpikes of wonder
Wine leads the mind forth,
Straight, sidewise, and upward,
West, southward, and north.

Stands the vault adamantine
Until the Doomsday;
The wine-cup shall ferry
Thee o'er it away.

I, a Wanderer

Oft have I said, I say it once more,
I, a wanderer, do not stray from myself.
I am a kind of parrot; the mirror is holden to me;
What the Eternal says, I stammering say again.
Give me what you will; I eat thistles as roses,
And according to my food I grow and I give.
Scorn me not, but know I have the pearl,
And am only seeking one to receive it.

* * *

Imagine how shocking it was more than 150 years ago for RWE to write of "Allah" as God, in this translated poem.

The Phoenix

My phoenix long ago secured
His nest in the sky-vault's cope;

In the body's cage immured,
He is weary of life's hope.

Round and round this heap of ashes
Now flies the bird amain,
But in that odorous niche of heaven
Nestles the bird again.

Once flies he upward, he will perch
On Tuba's golden bough;
His home is on that fruited arch
Which cools the blest below.

If over this world of ours
His wings my phoenix spread,
How gracious falls on land and sea
The soul-refreshing shade!

Either world inhabits he,
Sees oft below him planets roll;
His body is all of air compact,
Of Allah's love his soul.

Source of Song

Ah, could I hide me in my song,
To kiss thy kips from which it flows!

My Heart Forgets to Pray

I know this perilous love-lane
No whither the traveller leads,
Yet my fancy the sweet scent of
Thy tangled tresses feeds.

In the midnight of thy locks,
I renounce the day;
In the ring of thy rose-lips,
My heart forgets to pray.

WRITINGS ON PRAYER

RWE was occupied throughout the late 1830s and early 1840s with reimagining every form of Christian faith and practice that he had formally embraced. His writings from this period are often combative, even angry, in a way that we don't see later in his life. RWE experienced condemnation at the hands of his Christian contemporaries in a way that is common in every era when a former believer moves into heterodoxy. This essay from The Dial, *"Prayers," first published in 1842, reproduced here in its entirety, shows RWE urging his contemporaries to move beyond the prayers of Christianity and to see spiritual lights in other traditions.*

Not with fond shekels of the tested gold,
Nor gems whose rates are either rich or poor,
As fancy values them: but with true prayers,
That shall be up at heaven, and enter there
Ere sunrise; prayers from preserved souls,
From fasting maids, whose minds are dedicate
To nothing temporal.

—Shakespeare

Pythagoras said that the time when men are honestest, is when they present themselves before the gods. If we can overhear the prayer, we shall know the man. But prayers are not made to be overheard, or to be printed, so that we seldom have the prayer otherwise than it can be inferred from the man and his fortunes, which are the answer to the prayer, and always accord with it. Yet there are scattered about in the earth a few records of these

devout hours which it would edify us to read, could they be collected in a more catholic spirit than the wretched and repulsive
volumes which usurp that name. Let us not have the prayers
of one sect, nor of the Christian Church, but of men in all ages
and religions, who have prayed well. The prayer of Jesus is, as
it deserves, become a form for the human race. Many men have
contributed a single expression, a single word to the language
of devotion, which is immediately caught and stereotyped in the
prayers of their church and nation. Among the remains of Eurip-
ides, we have this prayer; "Thou God of all! Infuse light into the
souls of men, whereby they may be enabled to know what is
the root from whence all their evils spring, and by what means
they may avoid them." In the Phaedrus of Plato, we find this
petition in the mouth of Socrates; "O gracious Pan! And ye other
gods who preside over this place! Grant that I may be beautiful
within; and that those external things, which I have, may be such
as may best agree with a right internal disposition of mind; and
that I may account him to be rich, who is wise and just." Wacic
the Caliph, who died A. D. 845, ended his life, the Arabian his-
torians tell us, with these words; "O thou whose kingdom never
passes away, pity one whose dignity is so transient." But what
led us to these remembrances was the happy accident which in
this undevoutage lately brought us acquainted with two or three
diaries which attest, if there be need of attestation, the eternity
of the sentiment and its equality to itself through all the variety
of expression. The first is the prayer of a deaf and dumb boy.

"When my long-attached friend comes to me, I have pleasure
to converse with him, and I rejoice to pass my eyes over his coun-
tenance; but soon I am weary of spending my time causelessly
and unimproved and I desire to leave him, (but not in rudeness,)
because I wish to be engaged in my business. But thou, O my
Father, knowest I always delight to commune with thee in my
lone and silent heart; I am never full of thee; I am never weary of
thee; I am always desiring thee. I hunger with strong hope and
affection for thee, and I thirst for thy grace and spirit.

"When I go to visit my friends, I must put on my best garments, and I must think of my manner to please them. I am tired
to stay long, because my mind is not free, and they sometimes
talk gossip with me. But, Oh my Father, thou visitest me in my
work, and I can lift up my desires to thee, and my heart is cheered
and at rest with thy presence, and I am always alone with thee,
and thou dost not steal my time by foolishness. I always ask in
my heart, where can I find thee?"

The next is a voice out of a solitude as strict and sacred as that
in which nature had isolated this eloquent mute.

"My Father, when I cannot be cheerful or happy, I can be true
and obedient, and I will not forget that joy has been, and may
still be. If there is no hour of solitude granted me, still I will commune with thee. If I may not search out and pierce my thought,
so much the more may my living praise thee. At whatever price, I
must be alone with thee; this must be the demand I make. These
duties are not the life, but the means which enable us to show
forth the life. So must I take up this cross, and bear it willingly.
Why should I feel reproved when a busy one enters the room? I
am not idle though I sit with folded hands; but instantly I must
seek some cover. For that shame I reprove myself. Are they only
the valuable members of society who labor to dress and feed
it? Shall we never ask the aim of all this hurry and foam, of
this aimless activity? Let the purpose for which I live be always
before me; let every thought and word go to confirm and illumi-
nate that end; namely, that I must become near and dear to thee;
that now I am beyond the reach of all but thee.

"How can we not be reconciled to thy will? I will know the
joy of giving to my friend the dearest treasure I have. I know that
sorrow comes not at once only. We cannot meet it, and say, now
it is overcome, but again, and yet again its flood pours over us,
and as full as at first.

> "If but this tedious battle could be fought,
>   Like Sparta's heroes at one rocky pass,

> `One day be spent in dying,' men had sought
> The spot and been cut down like mower's grass."

The next is in a metrical form. It is the aspiration of a different mind, in quite other regions of power and duty, yet they all
accord at last.

> "Great God, I ask thee for no meaner pelf
> Than that I may not disappoint myself,
> That in my action I may soar as high,
> As I can now discern with this clear eye.
> And next in value, which they kindness lends,
> That I may greatly disappoint my friends,
> Howe'er they think or hope that it may be,
> They may not dream how thou'st distinguished me.
> That my weak hand may equal my firm faith,
> And my life practise more than my tongue saith;
> That my low conduct may not show,
> Nor my relenting lines,
> That I thy purpose did not know,
> Or overrated thy designs."

The last of the four orisons is written in a singularly calm and
healthful spirit, and contains this petition.

"My Father! I now come to thee with a desire to thank thee
for the continuance of our love, the one for the other. I feel that
without thy love in me, I should be alone here in the flesh. I cannot express my gratitude for what thou hast been and contin-
uest to be to me. But thou knowest what my feelings are. When
nought on earth seemeth pleasant to me, thou dost make thyself
known to me, and teach me that which is needful for me, and
dost cheer my travels on. I know that thou hast not created me
and placed me here on earth, amidst its toils and troubles, and
the follies of those around me, and told me to be like thyself,
when I see so little of thee here to profit by; thou hast not done

this, and then left me to myself, a poor, weak man, scarcely able to earn my bread. No; thou art my Father, and I will love thee, for thou didst first love me, and lovest me still. We will ever be parent and child. Wilt thou give me strength to persevere in this great work of redemption. Wilt thou show me the true means of accomplishing it. . . . I thank thee for the knowledge that I have attained of thee by thy sons who have been before me, and especially for him who brought me so perfect a type of thy goodness and love to men. . . . I know that thou wilt deal with me as I deserve. I place myself therefore in thy hand, knowing that thou wilt keep me from all harm so long as I consent to live under thy protecting care."

Let these few scattered leaves, which a chance, (as men say, but which to us shall be holy,) brought under our eye nearly at the same moment, stand as an example of innumerable similar expressions which no mortal witness has reported, and be a sign of the times. Might they be suggestion to many a heart of yet higher secret experiences which are ineffable! But we must not tie up the rosary on which we have strung these few white beads, without adding a pearl of great price from that book of prayer, the "Confessions of Saint Augustine."

"And being admonished to reflect upon myself, I entered into the very inward parts of my soul, by thy conduct; and I was able to do it, because now thou wert become my helper. I entered and discerned with the eye of my soul, (such as it was,) even beyond my soul and mind itself the Light unchangeable. Not this vulgar light which all flesh may look upon, nor as it were a greater of the same kind, as though the brightness of this should be manifold greater and with its greatness take up all space. Not such was this light, but other, yea, far other from all these. Neither was it so above my understanding, as oil swims above water, or as the heaven is above the earth. But it is above me, because it made me; and I am under it, because I was made by it. He that knows truth or verity, knows what that Light is, and he that

knows it knows eternity, and it is known by charity. O eternal
Verity! And true Charity! And dear Eternity! Thou art my God,
to thee do I sigh day and night. Thee when I first knew, thou
liftedst me up that I might see there was what I might see, and
that I was not yet such as to see. And thou didst beat back my
weak sight upon myself, shooting out beams upon me after a
vehement manner, and I even trembled between love and horror,
and I found myself to be far off, and even in the very region of
dissimilitude from thee."

* * *

*This short passage from "Self-Reliance" attempts to release
prayer from beseeching a deity to empowering the will and
actions of everyday people.*

In what prayers do men allow themselves! That which they call
a holy office is not so much as brave and manly. Prayer looks
abroad and asks for some foreign addition to come through
some foreign virtue, and loses itself in endless mazes of natural
and supernatural, and mediatorial and miraculous. Prayer that
craves a particular commodity,—any thing less than all good,—
is vicious. Prayer is the contemplation of the facts of life from
the highest point of view. It is the soliloquy of a beholding and
jubilant soul. It is the spirit of God pronouncing his works good.
But prayer as a means to effect a private end is meanness and
theft. It supposes dualism and not unity in nature and consciousness. As soon as the man is at one with God, he will not beg. He
will then see prayer in all action. . . .

Another sort of false prayers are our regrets. Discontent is
the want of self-reliance: it is infirmity of will. Regret calamities,
if you can thereby help the sufferer; if not, attend your own
work, and already the evil begins to be repaired. Our sympathy is just as base. We come to them who weep foolishly, and
sit down and cry for company, instead of imparting to them
truth and health in rough electric shocks, putting them once

more in communication with their own reason. The secret of fortune is joy in our hands. Welcome evermore to gods and men is the self-helping man. For him all doors are flung wide: him all tongues greet, all honors crown, all eyes follow with desire. Our love goes out to him and embraces him, because he did not need it. We solicitously and apologetically caress and celebrate him, because he held on his way and scorned our disapprobation. The gods love him because men hated him. "To the persevering mortal," said Zoroaster, "the blessed Immortals are swift."

As men's prayers are a disease of the will, so are their creeds a disease of the intellect. . . . Everywhere I am hindered of meeting God in my brother, because he has shut his own temple doors, and recites fables merely of his brother's, or his brother's brother's God. Every new mind is a new classification.

3

"A Wise Skepticism" (Stoic Values)

We hear "stoic" as a negative trait today; not so, in RWE's mind or era, when to be Stoic was to connect with a spiritual tradition reaching back to antiquity. "The Stoic view of the universe is colored by optimism," writes one expert a generation after RWE. "All comes from God, all works towards good." Sin, meanwhile, "is due to a lack of moral force, a want of tone in the moral sinews, an unhealthy condition of the soul."[33] In these ways, RWE was a man of deeply held Stoic beliefs and values.

OUR IDENTITY WITH THE FIRST CAUSE

This is what we might call the metaphysics of RWE's stoicism. From "Experience," Essays: Second.

If I have described life as a flux of moods, I must now add, that there is that in us which changes not, and which ranks all sensations and states of mind. The consciousness in each man is a sliding scale, which identifies him now with the First Cause, and now with the flesh of his body; life above life, in infinite degrees. The sentiment from which it sprung determines the dignity of any deed, and the question ever is, not, what you have done or forborne, but, at whose command you have done or forborne it.

Fortune, Minerva, Muse, Holy Ghost,—these are quaint names, too narrow to cover this unbounded substance. The baffled intellect must still kneel before this cause, which refuses to be named,—ineffable cause, which every fine genius has essayed to represent by some emphatic symbol, as, Thales by water, Anaximenes by air, Anaxagoras by (Nous) thought, Zoroaster by fire, Jesus and the moderns by love: and the metaphor of each has become a national religion. The Chinese Mencius has not been the least successful in his generalization. "I fully understand language," he said, "and nourish well my vast-flowing vigor."—"I beg to ask what you call vast-flowing vigor?"—said his companion. "The explanation," replied Mencius, "is difficult. This vigor is supremely great, and in the highest degree unbending. Nourish it correctly, and do it no injury, and it will fill up the vacancy between heaven and earth. This vigor accords with and assists justice and reason, and leaves no hunger."—In our more correct writing, we give to this generalization the name of Being, and thereby confess that we have arrived as far as we can go. Suffice it for the joy of the universe, that we have not arrived at a wall, but at interminable oceans. Our life seems not present, so much as prospective; not for the affairs on which it is wasted, but as a hint of this vast-flowing vigor. Most of life seems to be mere advertisement of faculty: information is given us not to sell ourselves cheap; that we are very great. So, in particulars, our greatness is always in a tendency or direction, not in an action. It is for us to believe in the rule, not in the exception. The noble are thus known from the ignoble. So in accepting the leading of the sentiments, it is not what we believe concerning the immortality of the soul, or the like, but the universal impulse to believe, that is the material circumstance, and is the principal fact in the history of the globe. Shall we describe this cause as that which works directly? The spirit is not helpless or needful of mediate organs. It has plentiful powers and direct effects. I am explained without explaining, I am felt without acting, and where I am not. Therefore all just persons are satisfied with their own praise. They refuse to explain themselves, and are content that new actions should do them that office. They believe that we communicate without speech, and above speech, and that no

right action of ours is quite unaffecting to our friends, at whatever distance; for the influence of action is not to be measured
by miles. Why should I fret myself, because a circumstance has
occurred, which hinders my presence where I was expected? If
I am not at the meeting, my presence where I am, should be
as useful to the commonwealth of friendship and wisdom, as
would be my presence in that place. I exert the same quality of
power in all places. Thus journeys the mighty Ideal before us;
it never was known to fall into the rear. No man ever came to
an experience which was satiating, but his good is tidings of a
better. Onward and onward! In liberated moments, we know
that a new picture of life and duty is already possible; the elements already exist in many minds around you, of a doctrine of
life which shall transcend any written record we have. The new
statement will comprise the skepticisms, as well as the faiths of
society, and out of unbeliefs a creed shall be formed. For, skepticisms are not gratuitous or lawless, but are limitations of the
affirmative statement, and the new philosophy must take them
in, and make affirmations out-side of them, just as much as it
must include the oldest beliefs.

"A WISE SKEPTICISM"

*This passage, from the opening pages of RWE's essay on Mon-
taigne, outlines the balance of perspective that RWE regularly
advocated for all healthy people. This relates to his urging of
combining the sensuous with the intellectual, faith that allows
doubt, and the physical and spiritual.*

Every fact is related on one side to sensation, and on the other
to morals. The game of thought is, on the appearance of one
of these two sides, to find the other: given the upper, to find
the under side. Nothing so thin but has these two faces, and
when the observer has seen the obverse, he turns it over to see
the reverse. Life is a pitching of this penny,—heads or tails. We

never tire of this game, because there is still a slight shudder of astonishment at the exhibition of the other face, at the contrast of the two faces. A man is flushed with success, and bethinks himself what this good luck signifies. He drives his bargain in the street; but it occurs that he also is bought and sold. He sees the beauty of a human face, and searches the cause of that beauty, which must be more beautiful. He builds his fortunes, maintains the laws, cherishes his children; but he asks himself, Why? and whereto? This head and this tail are called, in the language of philosophy, Infinite and Finite; Relative and Absolute; Apparent and Real; and many fine names beside.

Each man is born with a predisposition to one or the other of these sides of nature; and it will easily happen that men will be found devoted to one or the other. One class has the perception of difference, and is conversant with facts and surfaces, cities and persons, and the bringing certain things to pass;—the men of talent and action. Another class have the perception of identity, and are men of faith and philosophy, men of genius.

Each of these riders drives too fast. Plotinus believes only in philosophers; Fenelon, in saints; Pindar and Byron, in poets. Read the haughty language in which Plato and the Platonists speak of all men who are not devoted to their own shining abstractions: other men are rats and mice. The literary class is usually proud and exclusive. The correspondence of Pope and Swift describes mankind around them as monsters; and that of Goethe and Schiller, in our own time, is scarcely more kind.

It is easy to see how this arrogance comes. The genius is a genius by the first look he casts on any object. Is his eye creative? Does he not rest in angles and colors, but beholds the design,—he will presently undervalue the actual object. In powerful moments, his thought has dissolved the works of art and nature into their causes, so that the works appear heavy and faulty. He has a conception of beauty which the sculptor cannot embody. Picture, statue, temple, railroad, steam-engine, existed first in an artist's mind, without flaw, mistake, or friction, which impair the executed models. So did the Church, the State, college, court, social circle, and all the institutions. It is not strange that these men, remembering what they have seen and hoped of ideas, should affirm disdainfully the superiority of ideas. Having at some time seen that the happy soul will carry all the arts in power, they say, Why cumber ourselves with superfluous realizations? and like dreaming beggars they assume to speak and act as if these values were already substantiated.

On the other part, the men of toil and trade and luxury,—the animal world, including the animal in the philosopher and poet also, and the practical world, including the painful drudgeries which are never excused to philosopher or poet any more than to the rest,—weigh heavily on the other side. The trade in our streets believes in no metaphysical causes, thinks nothing of the force which necessitated traders and a trading planet to exist: no, but sticks to cotton, sugar, wool and salt. The ward meetings, on election days, are not softened by any misgiving of the value of these ballotings. Hot life is streaming in a single direction. To the men of this world, to the animal strength and spirits, to the men of practical power, whilst immersed in it, the man of ideas appears out of his reason. They alone have reason.

Things always bring their own philosophy with them, that is, prudence. No man acquires property without acquiring with it a little arithmetic also. In England, the richest country that ever existed, property stands for more, compared with personal ability, than in any other. After dinner, a man believes less, denies more: verities have lost some charm. After dinner, arithmetic is the only science: ideas are disturbing, incendiary, follies of young men, repudiated by the solid portion of society: and a man comes to be valued by his athletic and animal qualities. Spence relates that Mr. Pope was with Sir Godfrey Kneller one day, when his nephew, a Guinea trader, came in. "Nephew," said Sir Godfrey, "you have the honor of seeing the two greatest men in the world." "I don't know how great men you may be," said the Guinea man, "but I don't like your looks. I have often bought a man much better than both of you, all muscles and bones, for ten guineas." Thus the men of the senses revenge themselves on the professors and repay scorn for scorn. The first had leaped to conclusions not yet ripe, and say more than is true; the others make themselves merry with the philosopher, and weigh man by the pound. . . .

The inconvenience of this way of thinking is that it runs into indifferentism and then into disgust. Life is eating us up. We shall be fables presently. Keep cool: it will be all one a hundred years hence. Life's well enough, but we shall be glad to get out of it, and they will all be glad to have us. Why should we fret and drudge? Our meat will taste to-morrow as it did yesterday, and we may at last have had enough of it. "Ah," said my languid gentleman at Oxford, "there's nothing new or true,—and no matter."

With a little more bitterness, the cynic moans; our life is like an ass led to market by a bundle of hay being carried before him; he sees nothing but the bundle of hay. "There is so much trouble in coming into the world," said Lord Bolingbroke, "and so much more, as well as meanness, in going out of it, that 'tis hardly worthwhile to be here at all." I knew a philosopher of this kidney who was accustomed briefly to sum up his experience of human nature in saying, "Mankind is a damned rascal": and the natural corollary is pretty sure to follow,—"The world lives by humbug, and so will I."

The abstractionist and the materialist thus mutually exasperating each other, and the scoffer expressing the worst of materialism, there arises a third party to occupy the middle ground between these two, the skeptic, namely. He finds both wrong by being in extremes. He labors to plant his feet, to be the beam of the balance. He will not go beyond his card. He sees the one-sidedness of these men of the street; he will not be a Gibeonite; he

stands for the intellectual faculties, a cool head and whatever
serves to keep it cool; no unadvised industry, no unrewarded
self-devotion, no loss of the brains in toil. Am I an ox, or a
dray?—You are both in extremes, he says. You that will have all
solid, and a world of pig-lead, deceive yourselves grossly. You
believe yourselves rooted and grounded on adamant; and yet, if
we uncover the last facts of our knowledge, you are spinning like
bubbles in a river, you know not whither or whence, and you are
bottomed and capped and wrapped in delusions.

Neither will he be betrayed to a book and wrapped in a gown.
The studious class are their own victims; they are thin and pale,
their feet are cold, their heads are hot, the night is without sleep,
the day a fear of interruption,—pallor, squalor, hunger and egotism. If you come near them and see what conceits they entertain,—they are abstractionists, and spend their days and nights
in dreaming some dream; in expecting the homage of society to
some precious scheme, built on a truth, but destitute of proportion in its presentment, of justness in its application, and of all
energy of will in the schemer to embody and vitalize it.

But I see plainly, he says, that I cannot see. I know that human
strength is not in extremes, but in avoiding extremes. I, at least,
will shun the weakness of philosophizing beyond my depth.
What is the use of pretending to powers we have not? What
is the use of pretending to assurances we have not, respecting
the other life? Why exaggerate the power of virtue? Why be an
angel before your time? These strings, wound up too high, will
snap. If there is a wish for immortality, and no evidence, why
not say just that? If there are conflicting evidences, why not state
them? If there is not ground for a candid thinker to make up
his mind, yea or nay,—why not suspend the judgment? I weary
of these dogmatizers. I tire of these hacks of routine, who deny
the dogmas. I neither affirm nor deny. . . . I will try to keep
the balance true. Of what use to take the chair and glibly rattle
off theories of society, religion and nature, when I know that

practical objections lie in the way, insurmountable by me and by my mates? Why so talkative in public, when each of my neighbors can pin me to my seat by arguments I cannot refute? Why pretend that life is so simple a game, when we know how subtle and elusive the Proteus is? Why think to shut up all things in your narrow coop, when we know there are not one or two only, but ten, twenty, a thousand things, and unlike? Why fancy that you have all the truth in your keeping? There is much to say on all sides.

Who shall forbid a wise skepticism, seeing that there is no practical question on which any thing more than an approximate solution can be had?

"OBEY THYSELF"

These selections from the 1838 "Divinity School Address" are not only emblematic of RWE's stoicism, but illustrate how that philosophical/religious tradition distinctively addresses the subject of evil in human life. Notice how many times the word, "evil," recurs, here, and in what contexts.

In this refulgent summer, it has been a luxury to draw the breath of life. The grass grows, the buds burst, the meadow is spotted with fire and gold in the tint of flowers. The air is full of birds, and sweet with the breath of the pine, the balm-of-Gilead, and the new hay. Night brings no gloom to the heart with its welcome shade. Through the transparent darkness the stars pour their almost spiritual rays. Man under them seems a young child, and his huge globe a toy. The cool night bathes the world as with a river, and prepares his eyes again for the crimson dawn. The mystery of nature was never displayed more happily. The corn and the wine have been freely dealt to all creatures, and the never-broken silence with which the old bounty goes forward, has not yielded yet one word of explanation. One is constrained to respect the perfection of this world, in which our senses converse. How wide; how rich; what invitation from every property it gives to every faculty of man! In its fruitful soils; in its navigable sea; in its mountains of metal and stone; in its forests of all woods; in its animals; in its chemical ingredients; in the powers and path of light, heat, attraction, and life, it is well worth the pith and heart of great men to subdue and enjoy it. The planters, the mechanics, the inventors, the astronomers, the builders of cities, and the captains, history delights to honor.

But when the mind opens, and reveals the laws which traverse the universe, and make things what they are, then shrinks the great world at once into a mere illustration and fable of this mind. What am I? and What is? asks the human spirit with a curiosity new-kindled, but never to be quenched. Behold these outrunning laws, which our imperfect apprehension can see tend this way and that, but not come full circle. Behold these infinite relations, so like, so unlike; many, yet one. I would study, I would know, I would admire forever. These works of thought have been the entertainments of the human spirit in all ages.

A more secret, sweet, and overpowering beauty appears to man when his heart and mind open to the sentiment of virtue. Then he is instructed in what is above him. He learns that his being is without bound; that, to the good, to the perfect, he is born, low as he now lies in evil and weakness. That which he venerates is still his own, though he has not realized it yet. He ought. He knows the sense of that grand word, though his analysis fails entirely to render account of it. When in innocency, or when by intellectual perception, he attains to say,—"I love the Right; Truth is beautiful within and without, forevermore. Virtue, I am thine: save me: use me: thee will I serve, day and night, in great, in small, that I may be not virtuous, but virtue;"—then is the end of the creation answered, and God is well pleased.

The sentiment of virtue is a reverence and delight in the presence of certain divine laws. It perceives that this homely game of life we play, covers, under what seem foolish details, principles that astonish. The child amidst his baubles, is learning the action of light, motion, gravity, muscular force; and in the game of human life, love, fear, justice, appetite, man, and God, interact. These laws refuse to be adequately stated. They will not be written out on paper, or spoken by the tongue. They elude our persevering thought; yet we read them hourly in each other's faces, in each other's actions, in our own remorse. The moral traits which are all globed into every virtuous act and thought,—in speech, we must sever, and describe or suggest by painful enumeration of many particulars. Yet, as this sentiment is the essence of all religion, let me guide your eye to the precise objects of the sentiment, by an enumeration of some of those classes of facts in which this element is conspicuous.

The intuition of the moral sentiment is an insight of the perfection of the laws of the soul. These laws execute themselves. They are out of time, out of space, and not subject to circumstance. Thus; in the soul of man there is a justice whose retributions are instant and entire. He who does a good deed, is instantly ennobled. He who does a mean deed, is by the action itself contracted. He who puts off impurity, thereby puts on purity. If a man is at heart just, then in so far is he God; the safety of God, the immortality of God, the majesty of God do enter into that man with justice. If a man dissemble, deceive, he deceives himself, and goes out of acquaintance with his own being. A man in the view of absolute goodness, adores, with total humility. Every step so downward, is a step upward. The man who renounces himself, comes to himself.

See how this rapid intrinsic energy worketh everywhere, righting wrongs, correcting appearances, and bringing up facts to a harmony with thoughts. Its operation in life, though slow to the senses, is, at last, as sure as in the soul. By it, a man is made the Providence to himself, dispensing good to his goodness, and evil to his sin. Character is always known. Thefts never enrich; alms never impoverish; murder will speak out of stone walls. The least admixture of a lie,—for example, the taint of vanity, the least attempt to make a good impression, a favorable appearance,—will instantly vitiate the effect. But speak the truth, and all nature and all spirits help you with unexpected furtherance. Speak the truth, and all things alive or brute are vouchers, and the very roots of the grass underground there, do seem to stir and move to bear you witness. See again the perfection of the Law as it applies itself to the affections, and becomes the law of society. As we are, so we associate. The good, by affinity, seek the good; the vile, by affinity, the vile. Thus of their own volition, souls proceed into heaven, into hell.

These facts have always suggested to man the sublime creed, that the world is not the product of manifold power, but of one will, of one mind; and that one mind is everywhere active, in each ray of the star, in each wavelet of the pool; and whatever opposes that will, is everywhere balked and baffled, because things are made so, and not otherwise. Good is positive. Evil is merely privative, not absolute: it is like cold, which is the privation of heat. All evil is so much death or nonentity. Benevolence is absolute and real. So much benevolence as a man hath, so much life hath he. For all things proceed out of this same spirit, which is differently named love, justice, temperance, in its different applications, just as the ocean receives different names on the several shores which it washes. All things proceed out of the same spirit, and all things conspire with it. Whilst a man seeks good ends, he is strong by the whole strength of nature. In so far as he roves from these ends, he bereaves himself of power, of auxiliaries; his being shrinks out of all remote channels, he becomes less and less, a mote, a point, until absolute badness is absolute death.

The perception of this law of laws awakens in the mind a sentiment which we call the religious sentiment, and which makes our highest happiness. Wonderful is its power to charm and to command. It is a mountain air. It is the embalmer of the world.

It is myrrh and storax, and chlorine and rosemary. It makes the sky and the hills sublime, and the silent song of the stars is it. By it, is the universe made safe and habitable, not by science or power. Thought may work cold and intransitive in things, and find no end or unity; but the dawn of the sentiment of virtue on the heart, gives and is the assurance that Law is sovereign over all natures; and the worlds, time, space, eternity, do seem to break out into joy.

This sentiment is divine and deifying. It is the beatitude of man. It makes him illimitable. Through it, the soul first knows itself. It corrects the capital mistake of the infant man, who seeks to be great by following the great, and hopes to derive advantages from another,—by showing the fountain of all good to be in himself, and that he, equally with every man, is an inlet into the deeps of Reason. When he says, "I ought;" when love warms him; when he chooses, warned from on high, the good and great deed; then, deep melodies wander through his soul from Supreme Wisdom. Then he can worship, and be enlarged by his worship; for he can never go behind this sentiment. In the sublimest flights of the soul, rectitude is never surmounted, love is never outgrown.

This sentiment lies at the foundation of society, and successively creates all forms of worship. The principle of veneration never dies out. Man fallen into superstition, into sensuality, is never quite without the visions of the moral sentiment. In like manner, all the expressions of this sentiment are sacred and permanent in proportion to their purity. The expressions of this sentiment affect us more than all other compositions. The sentences of the oldest time, which ejaculate this piety, are still fresh and fragrant. This thought dwelled always deepest in the minds of men in the devout and contemplative East; not alone in Palestine, where it reached its purest expression, but in Egypt, in Persia, in India, in China. Europe has always owed to oriental genius, its divine impulses. What these holy bards said, all

sane men found agreeable and true. And the unique impression
of Jesus upon mankind, whose name is not so much written as
ploughed into the history of this world, is proof of the subtle
virtue of this infusion.

Meantime, whilst the doors of the temple stand open, night
and day, before every man, and the oracles of this truth cease
never, it is guarded by one stern condition; this, namely; it is an
intuition. It cannot be received at second hand. Truly speaking,
it is not instruction, but provocation, that I can receive from
another soul. What he announces, I must find true in me, or
wholly reject; and on his word, or as his second, be he who he
may, I can accept nothing. On the contrary, the absence of this
primary faith is the presence of degradation. As is the flood so
is the ebb. Let this faith depart, and the very words it spake,
and the things it made, become false and hurtful. Then falls
the church, the state, art, letters, life. The doctrine of the divine
nature being forgotten, a sickness infects and dwarfs the constitution. Once man was all; now he is an appendage, a nuisance.
And because the indwelling Supreme Spirit cannot wholly be got
rid of, the doctrine of it suffers this perversion, that the divine
nature is attributed to one or two persons, and denied to all the
rest, and denied with fury. The doctrine of inspiration is lost; the
base doctrine of the majority of voices, usurps the place of the
doctrine of the soul. Miracles, prophecy, poetry; the ideal life,
the holy life, exist as ancient history merely; they are not in the
belief, nor in the aspiration of society; but, when suggested, seem
ridiculous. Life is comic or pitiful, as soon as the high ends of
being fade out of sight, and man becomes near-sighted, and can
only attend to what addresses the senses.

These general views, which, whilst they are general, none will
contest, find abundant illustration in the history of religion, and
especially in the history of the Christian church. In that, all of
us have had our birth and nurture. The truth contained in that,
you, my young friends, are now setting forth to teach. As the

Cultus, or established worship of the civilized world, it has great historical interest for us. Of its blessed words, which have been the consolation of humanity, you need not that I should speak. I shall endeavor to discharge my duty to you, on this occasion, by pointing out two errors in its administration, which daily appear more gross from the point of view we have just now taken.

Jesus Christ belonged to the true race of prophets. He saw with open eye the mystery of the soul. Drawn by its severe harmony, ravished with its beauty, he lived in it, and had his being there. Alone in all history, he estimated the greatness of man. One man was true to what is in you and me. He saw that God incarnates himself in man, and evermore goes forth anew to take possession of his world. He said, in this jubilee of sublime emotion, "I am divine. Through me, God acts; through me, speaks. Would you see God, see me; or, see thee, when thou also thinkest as I now think." But what a distortion did his doctrine and memory suffer in the same, in the next, and the following ages! There is no doctrine of the Reason which will bear to be taught by the Understanding. The understanding caught this high chant from the poet's lips, and said, in the next age, "This was Jehovah come down out of heaven. I will kill you, if you say he was a man." The idioms of his language, and the figures of his rhetoric, have usurped the place of his truth; and churches are not built on his principles, but on his tropes. Christianity became a Mythus, as the poetic teaching of Greece and of Egypt, before. He spoke of miracles; for he felt that man's life was a miracle, and all that man doth, and he knew that this daily miracle shines, as the character ascends. But the word Miracle, as pronounced by Christian churches, gives a false impression; it is Monster. It is not one with the blowing clover and the falling rain.

He felt respect for Moses and the prophets; but no unfit tenderness at postponing their initial revelations, to the hour and the man that now is; to the eternal revelation in the heart. Thus was he a true man. Having seen that the law in us is commanding, he would not suffer it to be commanded. Boldly, with hand, and heart, and life, he declared it was God. Thus is he, as I think, the only soul in history who has appreciated the worth of a man.

In this point of view we become very sensible of the first defect of historical Christianity. Historical Christianity has fallen into the error that corrupts all attempts to communicate religion. As it appears to us, and as it has appeared for ages, it is not the doctrine of the soul, but an exaggeration of the personal, the positive, the ritual. It has dwelt, it dwells, with noxious exaggeration about the person of Jesus. The soul knows no persons. It invites every man to expand to the full circle of the universe, and will have no preferences but those of spontaneous love. But by this eastern monarchy of a Christianity, which indolence and fear have built, the friend of man is made the injurer of man. The manner in which his name is surrounded with expressions, which were once sallies of admiration and love, but are now petrified into official titles, kills all generous sympathy and liking. All who hear me, feel, that the language that describes Christ to Europe and America, is not the style of friendship and enthusiasm to a good and noble heart, but is appropriated and formal,—paints a demigod, as the Orientals or the Greeks would describe Osiris or Apollo. Accept the injurious impositions of our early catechetical instruction, and even honesty and self-denial were but splendid sins, if they did not wear the Christian name. One would rather be

"A pagan, suckled in a creed outworn,"

than to be defrauded of his manly right in coming into nature, and finding not names and places, not land and professions, but even virtue and truth foreclosed and monopolized. You shall not be a man even. You shall not own the world; you shall not dare, and live after the infinite Law that is in you, and in company with the infinite Beauty which heaven and earth reflect to you in all lovely forms; but you must subordinate your nature to

Christ's nature; you must accept our interpretations; and take his portrait as the vulgar draw it.

That is always best which gives me to myself. The sublime is excited in me by the great stoical doctrine, Obey thyself. That which shows God in me, fortifies me. That which shows God out of me, makes me a wart and a wen. There is no longer a necessary reason for my being. Already the long shadows of untimely oblivion creep over me, and I shall decease forever.

The divine bards are the friends of my virtue, of my intellect of my strength. They admonish me, that the gleams which flash across my mind, are not mine, but God's; that they had the like, and were not disobedient to the heavenly vision. So I love them. Noble provocations go out from them, inviting me to resist evil; to subdue the world; and to Be. And thus by his holy thoughts, Jesus serves us, and thus only. To aim to convert a man by miracles, is a profanation of the soul. A true conversion, a true Christ, is now, as always, to be made, by the reception of beautiful sentiments. It is true that a great and rich soul, like his, falling among the simple, does so preponderate, that, as his did, it names the world. The world seems to them to exist for him, and they have not yet drunk so deeply of his sense, as to see that only by coming again to themselves, or to God in themselves, can they grow forevermore. It is a low benefit to give me something; it is a high benefit to enable me to do somewhat of myself. The time is coming when all men will see, that the gift of God to the soul is not a vaunting, overpowering, excluding sanctity, but a sweet, natural goodness, a goodness like thine and mine, and that so invites thine and mine to be and to grow.

The injustice of the vulgar tone of preaching is not less flagrant to Jesus, than to the souls which it profanes. The preachers do not see that they make his gospel not glad, and shear him of the locks of beauty and the attributes of heaven. When I see a majestic Epaminondas, or Washington; when I see among my contemporaries, a true orator, an upright judge, a dear friend;

when I vibrate to the melody and fancy of a poem; I see beauty that is to be desired. And so lovely, and with yet more entire consent of my human being, sounds in my ear the severe music of the bards that have sung of the true God in all ages. Now do not degrade the life and dialogues of Christ out of the circle of this charm, by insulation and peculiarity. Let them lie as they befel, alive and warm, part of human life, and of the landscape, and of the cheerful day.

"TRUST THYSELF"

William James probably captured RWE's radical spiritual thought best when he summarized it: "Cleave ever to God . . . against your Creator."[34] *This is similar to the Buddhist notion of "If you ever meet the Buddha on the road, kill him," and it captures the iconoclasm of this essay well. From "Self-Reliance."*

I read the other day some verses written by an eminent painter which were original and not conventional. The soul always hears an admonition in such lines, let the subject be what it may. The sentiment they instil is of more value than any thought they may contain. To believe your own thought, to believe that what is true for you in your private heart is true for all men,—that is genius. Speak your latent conviction, and it shall be the universal sense; for the inmost in due time becomes the outmost,—and our first thought is rendered back to us by the trumpets of the Last Judgment. Familiar as the voice of the mind is to each, the highest merit we ascribe to Moses, Plato, and Milton is, that they set at naught books and traditions, and spoke not what men but what they thought. A man should learn to detect and watch that gleam of light which flashes across his mind from within, more than the lustre of the firmament of bards and sages. Yet he dismisses without notice his thought, because it is his. In every work of genius we recognize our own rejected thoughts: they come back to us with a certain alienated majesty. Great works of art have no more affecting lesson for us than this. They teach us to abide by our spontaneous impression with good-humored inflexibility then most when the whole cry of voices is on the other side. Else, tomorrow a stranger will say with masterly good sense precisely what we have thought and felt all the time, and we shall be forced to take with shame our own opinion from another.

There is a time in every man's education when he arrives at the conviction that envy is ignorance; that imitation is suicide; that he must take himself for better, for worse, as his portion; that though the wide universe is full of good, no kernel of nourishing corn can come to him but through his toil bestowed on that plot of ground which is given to him to till. The power which resides in him is new in nature, and none but he knows what that is which he can do, nor does he know until he has tried. Not for nothing one face, one character, one fact, makes much impression on him, and another none. This sculpture in the memory is not without pre-established harmony. The eye was placed where one ray should fall, that it might testify of that particular ray. We but half express ourselves, and are ashamed of that divine idea which each of us represents. It may be safely trusted as proportionate and of good issues, so it be faithfully imparted, but God will not have his work made manifest by cowards. A man is relieved and gay when he has put his heart into his work and done his best; but what he has said or done otherwise, shall give him no peace. It is a deliverance which does not deliver. In the attempt his genius deserts him; no muse befriends; no invention, no hope.

Trust thyself: every heart vibrates to that iron string. Accept the place the divine providence has found for you, the society of your contemporaries, the connection of events. Great men have always done so, and confided themselves childlike to the genius of their age, betraying their perception that the absolutely trustworthy was seated at their heart, working through their hands, predominating in all their being. And we are now men, and must accept in the highest mind the same transcendent destiny; and not minors and invalids in a protected corner, not cowards fleeing before a revolution, but guides, redeemers, and benefactors, obeying the Almighty effort, and advancing on Chaos and the Dark.

The other terror that scares us from self-trust is our consistency; a reverence for our past act or word, because the eyes of others have no other data for computing our orbit than our past acts, and we are loath to disappoint them.

But why should you keep your head over your shoulder? Why drag about this corpse of your memory, lest you contradict somewhat you have stated in this or that public place? Suppose you should contradict yourself; what then? It seems to be a rule of wisdom never to rely on your memory alone, scarcely even in acts of pure memory, but to bring the past for judgment into the thousand-eyed present, and live ever in a new day. In your metaphysics you have denied personality to the Deity: yet when the devout motions of the soul come, yield to them heart and life, though they should clothe God with shape and color. Leave your theory, as Joseph his coat in the hand of the harlot, and flee.

A foolish consistency is the hobgoblin of little minds, adored by little statesmen and philosophers and divines. With consistency a great soul has simply nothing to do. He may as well concern himself with his shadow on the wall. Speak what you think now in hard words, and to-morrow speak what to-morrow thinks in hard words again, though it contradict every thing you said to-day.—"Ah, so you shall be sure to be misunderstood."—Is it so bad, then, to be misunderstood? Pythagoras was misunderstood, and Socrates, and Jesus, and Luther, and Copernicus, and Galileo, and Newton, and every pure and wise spirit that ever took flesh. To be great is to be misunderstood.

"THE WHOLE COURSE OF THINGS GOES TO TEACH US FAITH"

RWE explains his belief that all is right with the world, and us—if we are aligned with the world. From "Spiritual Laws," Essays: First.

A little consideration of what takes place around us every day would show us, that a higher law than that of our will regulates events; that our painful labors are unnecessary, and fruitless; that only in our easy, simple, spontaneous action are we strong, and by contenting ourselves with obedience we become divine. Belief and love,—a believing love will relieve us of a vast load of care. O my brothers, God exists. There is a soul at the center of nature, and over the will of every man, so that none of us can wrong the universe. It has so infused its strong enchantment into nature, that we prosper when we accept its advice, and when we struggle to wound its creatures, our hands are glued to our sides, or they beat our own breasts. The whole course of things goes to teach us faith. We need only obey. There is guidance for each of us, and by lowly listening we shall hear the right word. Why need you choose so painfully your place, and occupation, and associates, and modes of action, and of entertainment? Certainly there is a possible right for you that precludes the need of balance and wilful election. For you there is a reality, a fit place and congenial duties. Place yourself in the middle of the stream of power and wisdom which animates all whom it floats, and you are without effort impelled to truth, to right, and a perfect contentment. Then you put all gainsayers in the wrong. Then you are the world, the measure of right, of truth, of beauty. If we will not be mar-plots with our miserable interferences, the work, the society, letters, arts, science, religion of men would go on far better than now, and the heaven predicted from the beginning of the world, and still predicted from the bottom of the heart, would organize itself, as do now the rose, and the air, and the sun.

"CHARACTER REMINDS YOU OF NOTHING"

Another brief selection from perhaps RWE's most famous writing. From "Self-Reliance," Essays: First.

I hope in these days we have heard the last of conformity and consistency. Let the words be gazetted and ridiculous henceforward. Instead of the gong for dinner, let us hear a whistle from the Spartan fife. Let us never bow and apologize more. A great man is coming to eat at my house. I do not wish to please him; I wish that he should wish to please me. I will stand here for humanity, and though I would make it kind, I would make it true. Let us affront and reprimand the smooth mediocrity and squalid contentment of the times, and hurl in the face of custom, and trade, and office, the fact which is the upshot of all history, that there is a great responsible Thinker and Actor working wherever a man works; that a true man belongs to no other time or place, but is the centre of things. Where he is, there is nature. He measures you, and all men, and all events. Ordinarily, every body in society reminds us of somewhat else, or of some other person. Character, reality, reminds you of nothing else; it takes place of the whole creation. The man must be so much, that he must make all circumstances indifferent. Every true man is a cause, a country, and an age; requires infinite spaces and numbers and time fully to accomplish his design. . . . Let a man then know his worth, and keep things under his feet.

"THE INDIFFERENCY OF CIRCUMSTANCES"

This passage is from the early essay, "Compensation."

Thus do all things preach the indifferency of circumstances. The man is all. Every thing has two sides, a good and an evil. Every advantage has its tax. I learn to be content. But the doctrine of compensation is not the doctrine of indifferency. The thoughtless say, on hearing these representations,—What boots it to do well? there is one event to good and evil; if I gain any good, I must pay for it; if I lose any good, I gain some other; all actions are indifferent.

There is a deeper fact in the soul than compensation, to wit, its own nature. The soul is not a compensation, but a life. The soul is. Under all this running sea of circumstance, whose waters ebb and flow with perfect balance, lies the aboriginal abyss of real Being. Essence, or God, is not a relation, or a part, but the whole. Being is the vast affirmative, excluding negation, self-balanced, and swallowing up all relations, parts, and times within itself. . . .

Such, also, is the natural history of calamity. The changes which break up at short intervals the prosperity of men are advertisements of a nature whose law is growth. Every soul is by this intrinsic necessity quitting its whole system of things, its friends, and home, and laws, and faith, as the shellfish crawls out of its beautiful but stony case, because it no longer admits of its growth, and slowly forms a new house. In proportion to the vigor of the individual, these revolutions are frequent, until in some happier mind they are incessant, and all worldly relations hang very loosely about him, becoming, as it were, a transparent fluid membrane through which the living form is seen, and not, as in most men, an indurated heterogeneous fabric of many dates, and of no settled character in which the man is imprisoned. Then there can be enlargement, and the man of today scarcely recognizes the man of yesterday. And such should be the outward biography of man in time, a putting off of dead circumstances day by day, as he renews his raiment day by day. But to us, in our lapsed estate, resting, not advancing, resisting, not cooperating with the divine expansion, this growth comes by shocks.

We cannot part with our friends. We cannot let our angels go. We do not see that they only go out, that archangels may come in. We are idolaters of the old. We do not believe in the riches of the soul, in its proper eternity and omnipresence. We do not believe there is any force in today to rival or recreate that beautiful yesterday. We linger in the ruins of the old tent, where once we had bread and shelter and organs, nor believe that the spirit can feed, cover, and nerve us again. We cannot again find aught so dear, so sweet, so graceful. But we sit and weep in vain. The voice of the Almighty saith, "Up and onward for evermore!" We cannot stay amid the ruins. Neither will we rely on the new; and so we walk ever with reverted eyes, like those monsters who look backwards.

And yet the compensations of calamity are made apparent to the understanding also, after long intervals of time. A fever, a mutilation, a cruel disappointment, a loss of wealth, a loss of friends, seems at the moment unpaid loss, and unpayable. But the sure years reveal the deep remedial force that underlies all facts. The death of a dear friend, wife, brother, lover, which seemed nothing but privation, somewhat later assumes the aspect of a guide or genius; for it commonly operates revolutions in our way of life, terminates an epoch of infancy or of youth which was waiting to be closed, breaks up a wonted occupation, or a household, or style of living, and allows the formation of new ones more friendly to the growth of character. It permits or constrains the formation of new acquaintances, and the reception of new influences that prove of the first importance to the next years; and the man or woman who would have remained a sunny garden-flower, with no room for its roots and too much sunshine for its head, by the falling of the walls and the neglect of the gardener, is made the banian of the forest, yielding shade and fruit to wide neighborhoods of men.

THREE POEMS ABOUT DEATH

This subject did not overly preoccupy RWE; in fact, you might say that he avoided it, perhaps because he grew up with an eccentric aunt, Mary Moody Emerson, who was both puritanical in outlook and obsessed with death (her bed was made like a coffin). However, RWE's mature life was also deeply touched by death—particularly the extremely premature death of his first, beloved wife, Ellen; his brothers, Edward and Charles; and his son, Waldo (all between 1831 and 1842). So, to death RWE on occasion turned, usually in his journals or in verse—as in these three poems published in Poems *in 1847.*

Dirge

Knows he who tills this lonely field
To reap its scanty corn,
What mystic fruit his acres yield
At midnight and at morn?

In the long sunny afternoon,
The plain was full of ghosts,
I wandered up, I wandered down,
Beset by pensive hosts.

The winding Concord gleamed below,
Pouring as wide a flood
As when my brothers long ago,
Came with me to the wood.

But they are gone,—the holy ones,
Who trod with me this lonely vale,
The strong, star-bright companions
Are silent, low, and pale.

My good, my noble, in their prime,
Who made this world the feast it was,
Who learned with me the lore of time,
    Who loved this dwelling-place.

They took this valley for their toy,
They played with it in every mood,
A cell for prayer, a hall for joy,
    They treated nature as they would.

They colored the horizon round,
Stars flamed and faded as they bade,
All echoes hearkened for their sound,
They made the woodlands glad or mad.

I touch this flower of silken leaf
Which once our childhood knew
Its soft leaves wound me with a grief
    Whose balsam never grew.

Hearken to yon pine warbler
    Singing aloft in the tree;
Hearest thou, O traveller!
    What he singeth to me?

Not unless God made sharp thine ear
    With sorrow such as mine,
Out of that delicate lay couldst thou
    The heavy dirge divine.

Go, lonely man, it saith,
They loved thee from their birth,
Their hands were pure, and pure their faith,
There are no such hearts on earth.

Ye drew one mother's milk,
One chamber held ye all;
A very tender history
Did in your childhood fall.

Ye cannot unlock your heart,
The key is gone with them;
The silent organ loudest chants
The master's requiem.

A Mountain Grave

Why fear to die
And let thy body lie
Under the flowers of June,
Thy body food
For the ground-worms' brood
And thy grave smiled on by the visiting moon.

Amid great Nature's halls
Girt in by mountain walls
And washed with waterfalls
It would please me to die,
Where every wind that swept my tomb
Goes loaded with a free perfume
Dealt out with a God's charity.

I should like to die in sweets,
A hill's leaves for winding-sheets,
And the searching sun to see
That I am laid with decency.
And the commissioned wind to sing
His mighty psalm from fall to spring
And annual tunes commemorate
Of Nature's child the common fate.

To J. W.

Set not thy foot on graves;
Hear what wine and roses say;
The mountain chase, the summer waves,
The crowded town, thy feet may well delay.

Set not thy foot on graves;
Nor seek to unwind the shroud
Which charitable Time
And Nature have allowed
To wrap the errors of a sage sublime.

Set not thy foot on graves;
Care not to strip the dead
Of his sad ornament,
His myrrh, and wine, and rings,

His sheet of lead,
And trophies buried:
Go, get them where he earned them when alive;
As resolutely dig or dive.

Life is too short to waste
In critic peep or cynic bark,
Quarrel or reprimand:
'T will soon be dark;
Up! mind thine own aim, and
God speed the mark!

ADMIRATION FOR PLUTARCH

In "Self-Reliance," RWE had written, "[A]ll history resolves itself very easily into the biography of a few stout and earnest persons," an idea he undoubtedly picked up from Thomas Carlyle. Certain people are turnkeys for the movements, events, and important moments upon which the world opens and closes, both men believed. RWE's essay on Plutarch, excerpted here, was written to accompany a new translation of the first-century Roman historian's famous Lives.

Plutarch was a philosopher himself, a proponent of the ideas of Plato, who sometimes argued vigorously with Stoics; however, particularly from the distance of 1,750 years, Plutarch's mind and manners often appear Stoic themselves. In fact, one of the most interesting things we know about his character—not mentioned in this excerpt but surely known to RWE—was the Greek historian's attitude toward death. When his infant daughter died, Plutarch wrote to his wife, urging her not to grieve excessively, nor long.[35]

We are always interested in the man who treats the intellect well. We expect it from the philosopher,—from Plato, Aristotle, Spinoza and Kant; but we know that metaphysical studies in any but minds of large horizon and incessant inspiration have their dangers. One asks sometimes whether a metaphysician can treat the intellect well. The central fact is the superhuman intelligence, pouring into us from its unknown fountain, to be received with religious awe, and defended from any mixture of our will. But this high Muse comes and goes; and the danger is that, when the Muse is wanting, the student is prone to supply its place with microscopic subtleties and logomachy. It is fatal to spiritual health to lose your admiration. "Let others wrangle," said St. Augustine; "I will wonder." Plato and Plotinus are enthusiasts, who honor the race; but the logic of the sophists and materialists, whether Greek or French, fills us with disgust. Whilst we expect this awe and reverence of the spiritual power from the philosopher in his closet, we praise it in the man of the world—the man who lives on quiet terms with existing institutions, yet indicates his perception of these high oracles; as do Plutarch, Montaigne, Hume and Goethe. These men lift themselves at once from the vulgar and are not the parasites of wealth.

Perhaps they sometimes compromise, go out to dine, make and take compliments; but they keep open the source of wisdom and health. Plutarch is uniformly true to this center. He had not lost his wonder. He is a pronounced idealist, who does not hesitate to say, like another Berkeley. "Matter is itself privation;" and again, "The Sun is the cause that all men are ignorant of Apollo, by sense with—drawing the rational intellect from that which is to that which appears." He thinks that "souls are naturally endowed with the faculty of prediction;" he delights in memory, with its miraculous power of resisting time. He thinks that "Alexander invaded Persia with greater assistance from Aristotle than from his father Philip." He thinks that "he who has ideas of his own is a bad judge of another man's, it being true that the Eleans would be the most proper judges of the Olympic games, were no Eleans gamesters." He says of Socrates, that he endeavored to bring reason and things together, and make truth consist with sober sense. He wonders with Plato at that nail of pain and pleasure which fastens the body to the mind. The mathematics give him unspeakable pleasure, but he chiefly liked that proportion which teaches us to account that which is just, equal; and not that which is equal, just.

ADMIRATION FOR THOREAU

It is well known that RWE and Thoreau were close, and that Thoreau was stimulated to his own career as a writer, reformer, and thinker by RWE's "American Scholar" address of 1837. What is less known is that, after Thoreau's early death, RWE never lost an opportunity to sing his praises—and the portrait he painted of his younger friend was a Stoic one. These samples from his Thoreau biographical sketch are taken from the portrait published in Sketches, *the year after RWE's death.*

He interrogated every custom, and wished to settle all his practice on an ideal foundation. He was a protestant á outrance, and few lives contain so many renunciations. He was bred to no profession; he never married; he lived alone; he never went to church; he never voted; he refused to pay a tax to the State; he ate no flesh, he drank no wine, he never knew the use of tobacco; and, though a naturalist, he used neither trap nor gun. He chose, wisely no doubt for himself, to be the bachelor of thought and Nature. He had no talent for wealth, and knew how to be poor without the least hint of squalor or inelegance. Perhaps he fell into his way of living without forecasting it much, but approved it with later wisdom. "I am often reminded," he wrote in his journal, "that if I had bestowed on me the wealth of Crœsus, my aims must be still the same, and my means essentially the same." He had no temptations to fight against, no appetites, no passions, no taste for elegant trifles. A fine house, dress, the manners and talk of highly cultivated people were all thrown away on him. He much preferred a good Indian, and considered these refinements as impediments to conversation, wishing to meet his companion on the simplest terms. He declined invitations to dinner-parties, because there each was in every one's way, and he could not meet the individuals to any purpose. "They make their pride," he said, "in making their dinner cost much; I make my pride in making my dinner cost little." When asked at table what dish he preferred, he answered, "The nearest." He did not like the taste of wine, and never had a vice in his life. He said,—"I have a faint recollection of pleasure derived from smoking dried lily-stems, before I was a man. I had commonly a supply of these. I have never smoked anything more noxious."

He chose to be rich by making his wants few, and supplying them himself. In his travels, he used the railroad only to get over so much country as was unimportant to the present purpose, walking hundreds of miles, avoiding taverns, buying a lodging in farmers' and fishermen's houses, as cheaper, and more agreeable to him, and because there he could better find the men and the information he wanted.

There was somewhat military in his nature, not to be subdued, always manly and able, but rarely tender, as if he did not
feel himself except in opposition. He wanted a fallacy to expose,
a blunder to pillory, I may say required a little sense of victory,
a roll of the drum, to call his powers into full exercise. It cost
him nothing to say No; indeed he found it much easier than to
say Yes. It seemed as if his first instinct on hearing a proposition
was to controvert it, so impatient was he of the limitations of
our daily thought. This habit, of course, is a little chilling to the
social affections; and though the companion would in the end
acquit him of any malice or untruth, yet it mars conversation.
Hence, no equal companion stood in affectionate relations with
one so pure and guileless. "I love Henry," said one of his friends,
"but I cannot like him; and as for taking his arm, I should as
soon think of taking the arm of an elm-tree."

"A SERENE PROVIDENCE" (ADMIRATION FOR LINCOLN)

*This is the final paragraph of the funeral oration delivered by
RWE in Concord on April 19, 1865, as the nation mourned the
assassination of President Abraham Lincoln. Here RWE demonstrates his Stoic's view of God. From* Miscellanies.

The ancients believed in a serene and beautiful Genius which
ruled in the affairs of nations; which, with a slow but stern justice,
carried forward the fortunes of certain chosen houses, weeding
out single offenders or offending families, and securing at last
the firm prosperity of the favorites of Heaven. It was too narrow a view of the Eternal Nemesis. There is a serene Providence
which rules the fate of nations, which makes little account of
time, little of one generation or race, makes no account of disas-
ters, conquers alike by what is called defeat or by what is called
victory, thrusts aside enemy and obstruction, crushes everything
immoral as inhuman, and obtains the ultimate triumph of the

best race by the sacrifice of everything which resists the moral laws of the world. It makes its own instruments, creates the man for the time, trains him in poverty, inspires his genius, and arms him for his task. It has given every race its own talent, and ordains that only that race which combines perfectly with the virtues of all shall endure.

"A NEW CHURCH FOUNDED ON MORAL SCIENCE"

This page (from "Worship") demonstrates RWE's tendency to enthusiasm for a new approach to religion and faith. It also demonstrates what critics have characterized as "the strategy of Emerson's essays, where each sentence is self-contained but repeats, in different terms, the same idea."[36] Like a good sermon.

And so I think that the last lesson of life, the choral song which rises from all elements and all angels, is, a voluntary obedience, a necessitated freedom. Man is made of the same atoms as the world is, he shares the same impressions, predispositions, and destiny. When his mind is illuminated, when his heart is kind, he throws himself joyfully into the sublime order, and does, with knowledge, what the stones do by structure.

The religion which is to guide and fulfill the present and coming ages, whatever else it be, must be intellectual. The scientific mind must have a faith which is science. "There are two things," said Mahomet, "which I abhor, the learned in his infidelities, and the fool in his devotions." Our times are impatient of both, and specially of the last. Let us have nothing now which is not its own evidence. There is surely enough for the heart and imagination in the religion itself. Let us not be pestered with assertions and half-truths, with emotions and snuffle.

There will be a new church founded on moral science, at first cold and naked, a babe in a manger again, the algebra and mathematics of ethical law, the church of men to come, without shawms, or psaltery, or sackbut; but it will have heaven and earth for its beams and rafters; science for symbol and illustration; it will fast enough gather beauty, music, picture, poetry. Was never stoicism so stern and exigent as this shall be. It shall send man home to his central solitude, shame these social, supplicating manners, and make him know that much of the time he must have himself to his friend. He shall expect no cooperation, he shall walk with no companion. The nameless Thought, the nameless Power, the superpersonal Heart,—he shall repose alone on that. He needs only his own verdict. No good fame can help, no bad fame can hurt him. The Laws are his consolers, the good Laws themselves are alive, they know if he have kept them, they animate him with the leading of great duty, and an endless horizon. Honor and fortune exist to him who always recognizes the neighborhood of the great, always feels himself in the presence of high causes.

4

"Live in the Present" (to Cultivate Virtue)

This is where RWE's thought comes full circle. All that the mature RWE believed is contained in these selections. As he grew older, he became less confident in book learning and more and more drawn to the living world outside his study, and as he explored the ideas of German idealism, as well as Eastern mysticism, they combined in his own post-Christian perspective that still always seemed to retain the tone of Christ in the Gospels.

"GREAT ACTION MUST DRAW ON THE SPIRITUAL NATURE"

In another trademark, long, seemingly breathless single paragraph, this one from "Goethe; or, the Writer," Representative Men, RWE articulates how a life of action without contemplation is worthless—or dangerous. He even, perhaps controversially, takes to task a couple of religious movements (Quakers and Shakers) who act seemingly without a contemplative spirit; in this, RWE resembles Carlyle in denigrating repetition within religion as mere "enthusiasm" without true spirituality. RWE finds the integrated active-contemplative life of Hinduism to be far healthier.

If I were to compare action of a much higher strain with a life of contemplation, I should not venture to pronounce with much confidence in favor of the former. Mankind have such a deep stake in inward illumination, that there is much to be said by the hermit or monk in defense of his life of thought and prayer. A certain partiality, a headiness and loss of balance, is the tax which all action must pay. Act, if you like,—but you do it at your peril. Men's actions are too strong for them. Show me a man who has acted and who has not been the victim and slave of his action. What they have done commits and enforces them to do the same again. The first act, which was to be an experiment, becomes a sacrament. The fiery reformer embodies his aspiration in some rite or covenant, and he and his friends cleave to the form and lose the aspiration. The Quaker has established Quakerism, the Shaker has established his monastery and his dance; and although each prates of spirit, there is no spirit, but repetition, which is anti-spiritual. But where are his new things of today? In actions of enthusiasm this drawback appears, but in those lower activities, which have no higher aim than to make us more comfortable and more cowardly; in actions of cunning, actions that steal and lie, actions that divorce the speculative from the practical faculty and put a ban on reason and sentiment, there is nothing else but drawback and negation. The Hindus write in their sacred books, "Children only, and not the learned, speak of the speculative and the practical faculties as two. They are but one, for both obtain the selfsame end, and the place which is gained by the followers of the one is gained by the followers of the other. That man seeth, who seeth that the speculative and the practical doctrines are one." For great action must draw on the spiritual nature. The measure of action is the sentiment from which it proceeds.

SKEPTICISM AND SPIRIT

This is RWE courageously speaking his mind and heart, even though it alienated him from the creeds, spiritual practice, and worship of his ancestors, friends, and neighbors. He believed that skepticism was of profound importance to a living faith. From "Worship," Conduct.

I have no fears of being forced in my own despite to play, as we say, the devil's attorney. I have no infirmity of faith; no belief that it is of much importance what I or any man may say: I am sure that a certain truth will be said through me, though I should be dumb, or though I should try to say the reverse. Nor do I fear skepticism for any good soul. A just thinker will allow full swing to his skepticism. I dip my pen in the blackest ink, because I am not afraid of falling into my inkpot. I have no sympathy with a poor man I knew, who, when suicides abounded, told me he dared not look at his razor. We are of different opinions at different hours, but we always may be said to be at heart on the side of truth.

I see not why we should give ourselves such sanctified airs. If the Divine Providence has hid from men neither disease, nor deformity, nor corrupt society, but has stated itself out in passions, in war, in trade, in the love of power and pleasure, in hunger and need, in tyrannies, literatures, and arts,—let us not be so nice that we cannot write these facts down coarsely as they stand, or doubt but there is a counter-statement as ponderous, which we can arrive at, and which, being put, will make all square. The solar system has no anxiety about its reputation, and the credit of truth and honesty is as safe; nor have I any fear that a skeptical bias can be given by leaning hard on the sides of fate, of practical power, or of trade, which the doctrine of Faith cannot down-weigh. The strength of that principle is not measured in ounces and pounds: it tyrannizes at the center of Nature. We may well give skepticism as much line as we can. The spirit will return, and fill us. It drives the drivers. It counterbalances any accumulations of power.

"LABOR IS GOD'S EDUCATION"

This excerpt comes from the midst of RWE's address to the Mechanics' Apprentices' Library Association in Boston on January 25, 1841—not the sort of gathering one usually associates with an intellectual. In the early 1840s, RWE would talk with most anyone about his reforming ideas; and he did not consider himself an "intellectual." These are, in fact, reforming principles that RWE insisted upon for himself and anyone who would make a living with their ideas, or by writing books.

As in all great writing of this kind, the author is speaking to himself as well as his audience. Five days before the lecture was first given, RWE wrote in his journal, "When I look at the sweeping sleet amid the pine woods, my sentences look very contemptible, & I think I will never write more."[37]

[T]he whole interest of history lies in the fortunes of the poor. Knowledge, Virtue, Power are the victories of man over his necessities, his march to the dominion of the world. Every man ought to have this opportunity to conquer the world for himself. Only such persons interest us, Spartans, Romans, Saracens, English, Americans, who have stood in the jaws of need, and have by their own wit and might extricated themselves, and made man victorious.

I do not wish to overstate this doctrine of labor, or insist that every man should be a farmer, any more than that every man should be a lexicographer. In general, one may say, that the husbandman's is the oldest, and most universal profession, and that where a man does not yet discover in himself any fitness for one work more than another, this may be preferred. But the doctrine of the Farm is merely this, that every man ought to stand in primary relations with the work of the world, ought to do it himself, and not to suffer the accident of his having a purse in his pocket, or his having been bred to some dishonorable and injurious craft, to sever him from those duties; and for this reason, that labor is God's education; that he only is a sincere learner, he only can become a master, who learns the secrets of labor, and who by real cunning extorts from nature its scepter.

Neither would I shut my ears to the plea of the learned professions, of the poet, the priest, the lawgiver, and men of study generally; namely, that in the experience of all men of that class, the amount of manual labor which is necessary to the maintenance of a family, indisposes and disqualifies for intellectual exertion. I know, it often, perhaps usually, happens, that where there is a fine organization apt for poetry and philosophy, that individual finds himself compelled to wait on his thoughts, to waste several days that he may enhance and glorify one; and is better taught by a moderate and dainty exercise, such as rambling in the fields, rowing, skating, hunting, than by the downright drudgery of the farmer and the smith. I would not quite forget the venerable counsel of the Egyptian mysteries, which declared that "there were two pairs of eyes in man, and it is requisite that the pair which are beneath should be closed, when the pair that are above them perceive, and that when the pair above are closed, those which are beneath should be opened." Yet I will suggest that no separation from labor can be without some loss of power and of truth to the seer himself; that, I doubt not, the faults and vices of our literature and philosophy, their too great fineness, effeminacy, and melancholy, are attributable to the enervated and sickly habits of the literary class. Better that the book should not be quite so good, and the bookmaker abler and better, and not himself often a ludicrous contrast to all that he has written.

"THE DIVINE PRESENCE WITHIN"

These paragraphs are taken from RWE's brief talk on May 30, 1867, at the founding meeting of the Free Religious Association in Boston. Taken from Miscellanies.

We are all very sensible—it is forced on us every day—of the feeling that churches are outgrown; that the creeds are outgrown; that a technical theology no longer suits us. It is not the ill will of people—no, indeed, but the incapacity for confining themselves there. The church is not large enough for the man; it cannot inspire the enthusiasm which is the parent of everything good in history, which makes the romance of history. For that enthusiasm you must have something greater than yourselves, and not less.

The child, the young student, finds scope in his mathematics and chemistry or natural history, because he finds a truth larger than he is; finds himself continually instructed. But, in churches, every healthy and thoughtful mind finds itself in something less; it is checked, cribbed, confined. And the statistics of the American, the English and the German cities, showing that the mass of the population is leaving off going to church, indicate the necessity, which should have been foreseen, that the Church should always be new and extemporized, because it is eternal and springs from the sentiment of men, or it does not exist. One wonders sometimes that the churches still retain so many votaries, when he reads the histories of the Church. There is an element of childish infatuation in them which does not exalt our respect for man. Read in Michelet, that in Europe, for twelve or fourteen centuries, God the Father had no temple and no altar. The Holy Ghost and the Son of Mary were worshipped, and in the thirteenth century the First Person began to appear at the side of his Son, in pictures and in sculpture, for worship, but only through favor of his Son. These mortifying puerilities abound in religious history. But as soon as every man is apprised of the Divine Presence within his own mind,—is apprised that the perfect law of duty corresponds with the laws of chemistry, of vegetation, of astronomy, as face to face in a glass; that the basis of duty, the order of society, the power of character, the wealth of culture, the perfection of taste, all draw their essence from this moral sentiment, then we have a religion that exalts, that commands all the social and all the private action.

"LIVE IN THE PRESENT"

This selection from "Self-Reliance" is a drumroll of exhortation, urging his listeners toward one of his most persistent themes: trusting themselves. Specifically, RWE wants his contemporaries to stop their reverence of the past, and of past authorities; or else they'll never find or hear their own true voices. In our own day, poet Mary Oliver has pointed to this theme as RWE's greatest gift to generations that followed him: "uncloseting of thought into the world's brilliant, perilous present." RWE gleaned it most of all from Goethe.[38]

The relations of the soul to the divine spirit are so pure, that it is profane to seek to interpose helps. It must be that when God speaketh he should communicate, not one thing, but all things; should fill the world with his voice; should scatter forth light, nature, time, souls, from the centre of the present thought; and new date and new create the whole. Whenever a mind is simple, and receives a divine wisdom, old things pass away,—means, teachers, texts, temples fall; it lives now, and absorbs past and future into the present hour. All things are made sacred by relation to it,—one as much as another. All things are dissolved to their centre by their cause, and, in the universal miracle, petty and particular miracles disappear. If, therefore, a man claims to know and speak of God, and carries you backward to the phraseology of some old mouldered nation in another country, in another world, believe him not. Is the acorn better than the oak which is its fullness and completion? Is the parent better than the child into whom he has cast his ripened being? Whence, then, this worship of the past? The centuries are conspirators against the sanity and authority of the soul. Time and space are but physiological colors which the eye makes, but the soul is

light; where it is, is day; where it was, is night; and history is an
impertinence and an injury, if it be any thing more than a cheerful apologue or parable of my being and becoming.

Man is timid and apologetic; he is no longer upright; he dares
not say 'I think,' 'I am,' but quotes some saint or sage. He is
ashamed before the blade of grass or the blowing rose. These
roses under my window make no reference to former roses or
to better ones; they are for what they are; they exist with God
today. There is no time to them. There is simply the rose; it is
perfect in every moment of its existence. Before a leaf-bud has
burst, its whole life acts; in the full-blown flower there is no
more; in the leafless root there is no less. Its nature is satisfied,
and it satisfies nature, in all moments alike. But man postpones
or remembers; he does not live in the present, but with reverted
eye laments the past, or, heedless of the riches that surround him,
stands on tiptoe to foresee the future. He cannot be happy and
strong until he too lives with nature in the present, above time.

This should be plain enough. Yet see what strong intellects
dare not yet hear God himself, unless he speak the phraseology of I know not what David, or Jeremiah, or Paul. We shall
not always set so great a price on a few texts, on a few lives.
We are like children who repeat by rote the sentences of gran-
dames and tutors, and, as they grow older, of the men of talents
and character they chance to see,—painfully recollecting the
exact words they spoke; afterwards, when they come into the
point of view which those had who uttered these sayings, they
understand them, and are willing to let the words go; for, at
any time, they can use words as good when occasion comes. If
we live truly, we shall see truly. It is as easy for the strong man
to be strong, as it is for the weak to be weak. When we have
new perception, we shall gladly disburden the memory of its
hoarded treasures as old rubbish. When a man lives with God,
his voice shall be as sweet as the murmur of the brook and the
rustle of the corn.

CHARACTER: "THE SOUL OF FATE"

First published in 1860, this is the first chapter, "Fate," of one of RWE's most popular works, The Conduct of Life—*a title that surely sounds more moralistic than it did in the middle of the nineteenth century. RWE was at the height of his international fame.*

When there is something to be done, the world knows how to get it done. The vegetable eye makes leaf, pericarp, root, bark, or thorn, as the need is; the first cell converts itself into stomach, mouth, nose, or nail, according to the want: the world throws its life into a hero or a shepherd; and puts him where he is wanted. Dante and Columbus were Italians, in their time: they would be Russians or Americans to-day. Things ripen, new men come. The adaptation is not capricious. The ulterior aim, the purpose beyond itself, the correlation by which planets subside and crystallize, then animate beasts and men, will not stop, but will work into finer particulars, and from finer to finest.

The secret of the world is, the tie between person and event. Person makes event, and event person. The "times," "the age," what is that, but a few profound persons and a few active persons who epitomize the times?—Goethe, Hegel, Metternich, Adams, Calhoun, Guizot, Peel, Cobden, Kossuth, Rothschild, Astor, Brunel, and the rest. The same fitness must be presumed between a man and the time and event, as between the sexes, or between a race of animals and the food it eats, or the inferior races it uses. He thinks his fate alien, because the copula is hidden. But the soul contains the event that shall befall it, for the event is only the actualization of its thoughts; and what we pray to ourselves for is always granted. The event is the print of your form. It fits you like your skin. What each does is proper to him. Events are the children of his body and mind. We learn that the soul of Fate is the soul of us, as Hafiz sings,

> Alas! Till now I had not known,
> My guide and fortune's guide are one.

All the toys that infatuate men, and which they play for,—houses, land, money, luxury, power, fame, are the selfsame thing, with a new gauze or two of illusion overlaid. And of all the drums and rattles by which men are made willing to have their heads broke, and are led out solemnly every morning to parade,—the most admirable is this by which we are brought to believe that events are arbitrary, and independent of actions. At the conjuror's, we detect the hair by which he moves his puppet, but we have not eyes sharp enough to descry the thread that ties cause and effect.

Nature magically suits the man to his fortunes, by making these the fruit of his character. Ducks take to the water, eagles to the sky, waders to the sea margin, hunters to the forest, clerks to counting-rooms, soldiers to the frontier. Thus events grow on the same stem with persons; are sub-persons. The pleasure of life is according to the man that lives it, and not according to the work or the place. Life is an ecstasy. We know what madness belongs to love,—what power to paint a vile object in hues of heaven. As insane persons are indifferent to their dress, diet, and other accommodations, and, as we do in dreams, with equanimity, the most absurd acts, so, a drop more of wine in our cup of life will reconcile us to strange company and work. Each creature puts forth from itself its own condition and sphere, as the slug sweats out its slimy house on the pear-leaf, and the woolly aphides on the apple perspire their own bed, and the fish its shell. In youth, we clothe ourselves with rainbows, and go as brave as the zodiac. In age, we put out another sort of perspiration,—gout, fever, rheumatism, caprice, doubt, fretting, and avarice.

A man's fortunes are the fruit of his character. A man's friends are his magnetisms. We go to Herodotus and Plutarch for examples of Fate; but we are examples. "*Quisque suos patimur manes.*" The tendency of every man to enact all that is in his constitution is expressed in the old belief, that the efforts which we make to escape from our destiny only serve to lead us into it: and I have noticed, a man likes better to be complimented on his position, as the proof of the last or total excellence, than on his merits.

A man will see his character emitted in the events that seem to meet, but which exude from and accompany him. Events expand with the character. As once he found himself among toys, so now he plays a part in colossal systems, and his growth is declared in his ambition, his companions, and his performance. He looks like a piece of luck, but is a piece of causation;—the mosaic, angulated and ground to fit into the gap he fills. Hence in each town there is some man who is, in his brain and performance, an explanation of the tillage, production, factories, banks, churches, ways of living, and society, of that town. If you do not chance to meet him, all that you see will leave you a little puzzled: if you see him, it will become plain. We know in Massachusetts who built New Bedford, who built Lynn, Lowell, Lawrence, Clinton, Fitchburg, Holyoke, Portland, and many another noisy mart. Each of these men, if they were transparent, would seem to you not so much men, as walking cities, and, wherever you put them, they would build one.

"WE MUST MAKE IT REAL"

This passage speaks for itself and demonstrates how RWE's thought was ahead of his time. Were he living in the early twenty-first century, rather than the middle nineteenth, he'd remain warmly welcomed in the fold of a progressive Christianity. From "Worship," Conduct.

To make our word or act sublime, we must make it real. It is our system that counts, not the single word or unsupported action. Use what language you will, you can never say anything but what you are. What I am, and what I think, is conveyed to you, in spite of my efforts to hold it back. What I am has been secretly conveyed from me to another, whilst I was vainly making up my mind to tell him it. He has heard from me what I never spoke.

As men get on in life, they acquire a love for sincerity, and somewhat less solicitude to be lulled or amused. In the progress of the character, there is an increasing faith in the moral sentiment, and a decreasing faith in propositions. Young people admire talents, and particular excellences. As we grow older, we value total powers and effects, as the spirit, or quality of the man. We have another sight, and a new standard; an insight which disregards what is done for the eye, and pierces to the doer; an ear which hears not what men say, but hears what they do not say.

There was a wise, devout man who is called, in the Catholic Church, St. Philip Neri, of whom many anecdotes touching his discernment and benevolence are told at Naples and Rome. Among the nuns in a convent not far from Rome, one had appeared, who laid claim to certain rare gifts of inspiration and prophecy, and the abbess advised the Holy Father, at Rome, of the wonderful powers shown by her novice. The Pope did not well know what to make of these new claims, and Philip coming in from a journey, one day, he consulted him. Philip undertook to visit the nun, and ascertain her character. He threw himself on his mule, all travel-soiled as he was, and hastened through the mud and mire to the distant convent. He told the abbess the wishes of his Holiness, and begged her to summon the nun without delay. The nun was sent for, and, as soon as she came into the apartment, Philip stretched out his leg all bespattered with mud, and desired her to draw off his boots. The young nun, who had become the object of much attention and respect, drew back with anger, and refused the office: Philip ran out of doors, mounted his mule, and returned instantly to the Pope; "Give yourself no uneasiness, Holy Father, any longer: here is no miracle, for here is no humility."

5

"Wise Ancient Woods" (Encountering the Holy)

RWE not only found solace in the natural world around him, but he believed it participated in divinity. And RWE sometimes became rhapsodic about the holy potential of exploring wooded areas. He wrote in one "prose sonnet" these words: "Wise are ye, O ancient woods! wiser than man.... Men have not language to describe one moment of your eternal life. This I would ask of you, o sacred Woods, when ye shall next give me somewhat to say, give me also the tune wherein to say it."[39] These selections expand upon that theme.

"I AM PART OR PARTICLE OF GOD"

This first passage from the chapter, "Nature," in the book titled Nature, is often the first text a student reads from the pen of RWE. He published the essay first in 1836, and it became the trumpet of the Transcendental movement, marked by a new understanding of the connection between nature and spirit. *RWE viewed this relationship between the created and spiritual worlds in nondualist terms, as One. He wrote in his journal from January 1841, "Are there not moments in the history of heaven when the human race was not counted by individuals but was only God in distribution, God rushing into multiform benefit? It is sublime to receive, sublime to love, but this lust of *imparting, as from us, the desire to be loved, the wish to be recognized as individuals, is finite, comes of a lower strain."*[40]

To go into solitude, a man needs to retire as much from his chamber as from society. I am not solitary whilst I read and write, though nobody is with me. But if a man would be alone, let him look at the stars. The rays that come from those heavenly worlds, will separate between him and what he touches. One might think the atmosphere was made transparent with this design, to give man, in the heavenly bodies, the perpetual presence of the sublime. Seen in the streets of cities, how great they are! If the stars should appear one night in a thousand years, how would men believe and adore; and preserve for many generations the remembrance of the city of God which had been shown! But every night come out these envoys of beauty, and light the universe with their admonishing smile.

The stars awaken a certain reverence, because though always present, they are inaccessible; but all natural objects make a kindred impression, when the mind is open to their influence. Nature never wears a mean appearance. Neither does the wisest man extort her secret, and lose his curiosity by finding out all her perfection. Nature never became a toy to a wise spirit. The flowers, the animals, the mountains, reflected the wisdom of his best hour, as much as they had delighted the simplicity of his childhood.

When we speak of nature in this manner, we have a distinct but most poetical sense in the mind. We mean the integrity of impression made by manifold natural objects. It is this which distinguishes the stick of timber of the woodcutter, from the tree of the poet. The charming landscape which I saw this morning, is indubitably made up of some twenty or thirty farms. Miller owns this field, Locke that, and Manning the woodland beyond. But none of them owns the landscape. There is a property in the horizon which no man has but he whose eye can integrate all the parts, that is, the poet. This is the best part of these men's farms, yet to this their warranty-deeds give no title.

To speak truly, few adult persons can see nature. Most persons do not see the sun. At least they have a very superficial seeing. The sun illuminates only the eye of the man, but shines into the eye and the heart of the child. The lover of nature is he whose inward and outward senses are still truly adjusted to each other; who has retained the spirit of infancy even into the era of manhood. His intercourse with heaven and earth, becomes part of his daily food. In the presence of nature, a wild delight runs through the man, in spite of real sorrows. Nature says,—he is my creature, and maugre all his impertinent griefs, he shall be glad with me. Not the sun or the summer alone, but every hour and season yields its tribute of delight; for every hour and change corresponds to and authorizes a different state of the mind, from breathless noon to grimmest midnight. Nature is a setting that fits equally well a comic or a mourning piece. In good health, the air is a cordial of incredible virtue. Crossing a bare common, in snow puddles, at twilight, under a clouded sky, without having in my thoughts any occurrence of special good fortune, I have enjoyed a perfect exhilaration. I am glad to the brink of fear. In the woods too, a man casts off his years, as the snake his slough, and at what period soever of life, is always a child. In the woods, is perpetual youth. Within these plantations of God, a decorum and sanctity reign, a perennial festival is dressed, and the guest sees not how he should tire of them in a thousand years. In the woods, we return to reason and faith. There I feel that nothing can befall me in life,—no disgrace, no calamity (leaving me my eyes,) which nature cannot repair. Standing on the bare ground,—my head bathed by the blithe air, and uplifted into infinite space,—all mean egotism vanishes. I become a transparent eyeball; I am nothing; I see all; the currents of the Universal Being circulate through me; I am part or particle of God. The name of the nearest friend sounds then foreign and accidental:

to be brothers, to be acquaintances,—master or servant, is then a trifle and a disturbance. I am the lover of uncontained and immortal beauty. In the wilderness, I find something more dear and connate than in streets or villages. In the tranquil landscape, and especially in the distant line of the horizon, man beholds somewhat as beautiful as his own nature.

The greatest delight which the fields and woods minister, is the suggestion of an occult relation between man and the vegetable. I am not alone and unacknowledged. They nod to me, and I to them. The waving of the boughs in the storm, is new to me and old. It takes me by surprise, and yet is not unknown. Its effect is like that of a higher thought or a better emotion coming over me, when I deemed I was thinking justly or doing right.

Yet it is certain that the power to produce this delight, does not reside in nature, but in man, or in a harmony of both. It is necessary to use these pleasures with great temperance. For, nature is not always tricked in holiday attire, but the same scene which yesterday breathed perfume and glittered as for the frolic of the nymphs, is overspread with melancholy today. Nature always wears the colors of the spirit. To a man laboring under calamity, the heat of his own fire hath sadness in it. Then, there is a kind of contempt of the landscape felt by him who has just lost by death a dear friend. The sky is less grand as it shuts down over less worth in the population.

* * *

This passage is from the "Spirit" chapter in Nature.

It is essential to a true theory of nature and of man, that it should contain somewhat progressive. Uses that are exhausted or that may be, and facts that end in the statement, cannot be all that is true of this brave lodging wherein man is harbored, and wherein all his faculties find appropriate and endless exercise. And all the uses of nature admit of being summed in one, which yields the activity of man an infinite scope. Through all its kingdoms, to the suburbs and outskirts of things, it is faithful to the cause whence it had its origin. It always speaks of Spirit. It suggests the absolute. It is a perpetual effect. It is a great shadow pointing always to the sun behind us.

The aspect of Nature is devout. Like the figure of Jesus, she stands with bended head, and hands folded upon the breast. The happiest man is he who learns from nature the lesson of worship.

Of that ineffable essence which we call Spirit, he that thinks most, will say least. We can foresee God in the coarse, and, as it were, distant phenomena of matter; but when we try to define and describe himself, both language and thought desert us, and we are as helpless as fools and savages. That essence refuses to be recorded in propositions, but when man has worshipped him intellectually, the noblest ministry of nature is to stand as the apparition of God. It is the organ through which the universal spirit speaks to the individual, and strives to lead back the individual to it.

When we consider Spirit, we see that the views already presented do not include the whole circumference of man. We must add some related thoughts.

Three problems are put by nature to the mind; What is matter? Whence is it? and Whereto? The first of these questions only, the ideal theory answers. Idealism saith: matter is a phenomenon, not a substance. Idealism acquaints us with the total disparity between the evidence of our own being, and the evidence of the world's being. The one is perfect; the other, incapable of any assurance; the mind is a part of the nature of things; the world is a divine dream, from which we may presently awake to the glories and certainties of day. Idealism is a hypothesis to account for nature by other principles than those of carpentry and chemistry. Yet, if it only deny the existence of matter, it does not satisfy the demands of the spirit. It leaves God out of me. It leaves me in the splendid labyrinth of my perceptions, to wander without end. Then the heart resists it, because it balks the affections in denying substantive being to men and women. Nature is so pervaded with human life, that there is something of humanity in all, and in every particular. But this theory makes nature foreign to me, and does not account for that consanguinity which we acknowledge to it.

Let it stand, then, in the present state of our knowledge, merely as a useful introductory hypothesis, serving to apprize us of the eternal distinction between the soul and the world.

But when, following the invisible steps of thought, we come to inquire, Whence is matter? and Whereto? many truths arise to us out of the recesses of consciousness. We learn that the highest is present to the soul of man, that the dread universal essence, which is not wisdom, or love, or beauty, or power, but all in one, and each entirely, is that for which all things exist, and that by which they are; that spirit creates; that behind nature, throughout nature, spirit is present; one and not compound, it does not act upon us from without, that is, in space and time, but spiritually, or through ourselves: therefore, that spirit, that is, the Supreme Being, does not build up nature around us, but puts it forth through us, as the life of the tree puts forth new branches and leaves through the pores of the old. As a plant upon the earth, so a man rests upon the bosom of God; he is nourished by unfailing fountains, and draws, at his need, inexhaustible power. Who can set bounds to the possibilities of man? Once inhale the upper air, being admitted to behold the absolute natures of justice and truth, and we learn that man has access to the entire mind of the Creator, is himself the creator in the finite. This view, which admonishes me where the sources of wisdom and power lie, and points to virtue as to

> "The golden key
> Which opes the palace of eternity,"

carries upon its face the highest certificate of truth, because it animates me to create my own world through the purification of my soul.

The world proceeds from the same spirit as the body of man. It is a remoter and inferior incarnation of God, a projection of God in the unconscious. But it differs from the body in one important respect. It is not, like that, now subjected to the human will. Its serene order is inviolable by us. It is, therefore, to us, the present expositor of the divine mind. It is a fixed point whereby we may measure our departure. As we degenerate, the contrast between us and our house is more evident. We are as much strangers in nature, as we are aliens from God. We do not understand the notes of birds. The fox and the deer run away from us; the bear and tiger rend us. We do not know the uses of more than a few plants, as corn and the apple, the potato and the vine. Is not the landscape, every glimpse of which hath a grandeur, a face of him? Yet this may show us what discord is between man and nature, for you cannot freely admire a noble landscape, if laborers are digging in the field hard by. The poet finds something ridiculous in his delight, until he is out of the sight of men.

* * *

In the concluding chapter of Nature, *"Prospects," RWE attempts to find a synthesis to a new understanding of human beings in how they relate to the created world and to God. He appeals to the English poet, George Herbert, the ancient philosopher Plato, and then, in this concluding passage, even to the Scholastic theologians of the Middle Ages, to proclaim an essential connection that is on the verge of being discovered.*

At present, man applies to nature but half his force. He works on the world with his understanding alone. He lives in it, and masters it by a penny-wisdom; and he that works most in it, is but a half-man, and whilst his arms are strong and his digestion good, his mind is imbruted, and he is a selfish savage. His relation to nature, his power over it, is through the understanding; as by manure; the economic use of fire, wind, water, and the mariner's needle; steam, coal, chemical agriculture; the repairs of the human body by the dentist and the surgeon. This is such a resumption of power, as if a banished king should buy his territories inch by inch, instead of vaulting at once into his throne. Meantime, in the thick darkness, there are not wanting gleams of a better light,—occasional examples of the action of man upon nature with his entire force,—with reason as well as understanding. Such examples are; the traditions of miracles in the earliest antiquity of all nations; the history of Jesus Christ; the achievements of a principle, as in religious and political revolutions, and in the abolition of the Slave-trade; the miracles of enthusiasm, as those reported of Swedenborg, Hohenlohe, and the Shakers; many obscure and yet contested facts, now arranged under the name of Animal Magnetism; prayer; eloquence; self-healing; and the wisdom of children. These are examples of Reason's momentary grasp of the scepter; the exertions of a power which exists not in time or space, but an instantaneous in-streaming causing power. The difference between the actual and the ideal force of man is happily figured by the schoolmen, in saying, that the knowledge of man is an evening knowledge, *vespertina cognitio*, but that of God is a morning knowledge, *matutina cognitio*.[41]

The problem of restoring to the world original and eternal beauty, is solved by the redemption of the soul. The ruin or the blank, that we see when we look at nature, is in our own eye. The axis of vision is not coincident with the axis of things, and so they appear not transparent but opaque. The reason why the world lacks unity, and lies broken and in heaps, is, because man is disunited with himself. He cannot be a naturalist, until he satisfies all the demands of the spirit. Love is as much its demand, as perception. Indeed, neither can be perfect without the other. In the uttermost meaning of the words, thought is devout, and devotion is thought. Deep calls unto deep. But in actual life, the marriage is not celebrated. There are innocent men who worship God after the tradition of their fathers, but their sense of duty has not yet extended to the use of all their faculties. And there are patient naturalists, but they freeze their subject under the wintry light of the understanding. Is not prayer also a study of truth,—a sally of the soul into the unfound infinite? No man ever prayed heartily, without learning something. But when a faithful thinker, resolute to detach every object from personal relations, and see it in the light of thought, shall, at the same time, kindle science with the fire of the holiest affections, then will God go forth anew into the creation.

It will not need, when the mind is prepared for study, to search for objects. The invariable mark of wisdom is to see the miraculous in the common. What is a day? What is a year? What is summer? What is woman? What is a child? What is sleep? To our blindness, these things seem unaffecting. We make fables to hide the baldness of the fact and conform it, as we say, to the higher law of the mind. But when the fact is seen under the light of an idea, the gaudy fable fades and shrivels. We behold the real higher law. To the wise, therefore, a fact is true poetry, and the most beautiful of fables. These wonders are brought to our own door. You also are a man. Man and woman, and their social life, poverty, labor, sleep, fear, fortune, are known to you. Learn that none of these things is superficial, but that each phenomenon has its roots in the faculties and affections of the mind. Whilst the abstract question occupies your intellect, nature brings it in the concrete to be solved by your hands. It were a wise inquiry for the closet, to compare, point by point, especially at remarkable crises in life, our daily history, with the rise and progress of ideas in the mind.

So shall we come to look at the world with new eyes. It shall answer the endless inquiry of the intellect,—What is truth? and of the affections,—What is good? by yielding itself passive to the educated Will. Then shall come to pass what my poet said; "Nature is not fixed but fluid. Spirit alters, moulds, makes it. The immobility or bruteness of nature, is the absence of spirit; to pure spirit, it is fluid, it is volatile, it is obedient. Every spirit

builds itself a house; and beyond its house a world; and beyond
its world, a heaven. Know then, that the world exists for you.
For you is the phenomenon perfect. What we are, that only can
we see. All that Adam had, all that Caesar could, you have and
can do. Adam called his house, heaven and earth; Caesar called
his house, Rome; you perhaps call yours, a cobbler's trade; a
hundred acres of ploughed land; or a scholar's garret. Yet line
for line and point for point, your dominion is as great as theirs,
though without fine names. Build, therefore, your own world. As
fast as you conform your life to the pure idea in your mind, that
will unfold its great proportions. A correspondent revolution in
things will attend the influx of the spirit. So fast will disagreeable
appearances, swine, spiders, snakes, pests, madhouses, prisons,
enemies, vanish; they are temporary and shall be no more seen.
The sordor and filths of nature, the sun shall dry up, and the
wind exhale. As when the summer comes from the south; the
snow-banks melt, and the face of the earth becomes green before
it, so shall the advancing spirit create its ornaments along its
path, and carry with it the beauty it visits, and the song which
enchants it; it shall draw beautiful faces, warm hearts, wise discourse, and heroic acts, around its way, until evil is no more
seen. The kingdom of man over nature, which cometh not with
observation,—a dominion such as now is beyond his dream of
God,—he shall enter without more wonder than the blind man
feels who is gradually restored to perfect sight."

"MY GIANT GOES WITH ME WHEREVER I GO"

*This short passage from "Self-Reliance" expresses RWE's belief
that all a person needs is within him or her, while simultaneously
placing a priority on where we are right now, without need to
seek elsewhere.*

Travelling is a fool's paradise. Our first journeys discover to us
the indifference of places. At home I dream that at Naples, at

Rome, I can be intoxicated with beauty, and lose my sadness. I pack my trunk, embrace my friends, embark on the sea, and at last wake up in Naples, and there beside me is the stern fact, the sad self, unrelenting, identical, that I fled from. I seek the Vatican, and the palaces. I affect to be intoxicated with sights and suggestions, but I am not intoxicated. My giant goes with me wherever I go.

But the rage of travelling is a symptom of a deeper unsoundness affecting the whole intellectual action. The intellect is vagabond, and our system of education fosters restlessness. Our minds travel when our bodies are forced to stay at home. We imitate; and what is imitation but the travelling of the mind? Our houses are built with foreign taste; our shelves are garnished with foreign ornaments; our opinions, our tastes, our faculties, lean, and follow the Past and the Distant. The soul created the arts wherever they have flourished. It was in his own mind that the artist sought his model. It was an application of his own thought to the thing to be done and the conditions to be observed. And why need we copy the Doric or the Gothic model? Beauty, convenience, grandeur of thought, and quaint expression are as near to us as to any, and if the American artist will study with hope and love the precise thing to be done by him, considering the climate, the soil, the length of the day, the wants of the people, the habit and form of the government, he will create a house in which all these will find themselves fitted, and taste and sentiment will be satisfied also.

Insist on yourself; never imitate. Your own gift you can present every moment with the cumulative force of a whole life's cultivation; but of the adopted talent of another, you have only an extemporaneous, half possession. That which each can do best, none but his Maker can teach him. No man yet knows what it is, nor can, till that person has exhibited it. Where is the master who could have taught Shakspeare? Where is the master who could have instructed Franklin, or Washington, or Bacon, or Newton? Every great man is a unique. . . . Do that which is assigned you, and you cannot hope too much or dare too much. There is at this moment for you an utterance brave and grand as that of the colossal chisel of Phidias, or trowel of the Egyptians, or the pen of Moses, or Dante, but different from all these. Not possibly will the soul all rich, all eloquent, with thousand-cloven tongue, deign to repeat itself; but if you can hear what these patriarchs say, surely you can reply to them in the same pitch of voice; for the ear and the tongue are two organs of one nature. Abide in the simple and noble regions of thy life, obey thy heart, and thou shalt reproduce the Foreworld again.

"THOUGHTS IN PARALLEL WITH CELESTIAL CURRENTS"

I include this selection because it is simply beautiful, poetry in prose; but also, this short passage from "Swedenborg; Or, the Mystic," in Representative Men, *articulates RWE's belief in the divine connection, and mystical possibilities, present whenever the human imagination is allowed to truly mingle with the natural world.*

The secret of heaven is kept from age to age. No imprudent, no sociable angel ever dropt an early syllable to answer the longings of saints, the fears of mortals. We should have listened on our knees to any favorite, who, by stricter obedience, had brought his thoughts into parallelism with the celestial currents and could hint to human ears the scenery and circumstance of the newly parted soul. But it is certain that it must tally with what is best in nature. It must not be inferior in tone to the already known works of the artist who sculptures the globes of the firmament and writes the moral law. It must be fresher than rainbows, stabler than mountains, agreeing with flowers, with tides and the rising and setting of autumnal stars. Melodious poets shall be hoarse as street ballads when once the penetrating key-note of nature and spirit is sounded,—the earth-beat, sea-beat, heart-beat, which makes the tune to which the sun rolls, and the globule of blood, and the sap of trees.

"THE DEITY OF MAN" (INTRODUCING TRANSCENDENTALISM)

This is one of the most read selections from the writings of RWE—his bold, eloquent introduction to the principles of Transcendentalism. This essay dates from January 1842.

The first thing we have to say respecting what are called new views here in New England, at the present time, is, that they are not new, but the very oldest of thoughts cast into the mould of these new times. The light is always identical in its composition, but it falls on a great variety of objects, and by so falling is first revealed to us, not in its own form, for it is formless, but in theirs; in like manner, thought only appears in the objects it classifies. What is popularly called Transcendentalism among us, is Idealism; Idealism as it appears in 1842. As thinkers, mankind have ever divided into two sects, Materialists and Idealists; the first class founding on experience, the second on consciousness; the first class beginning to think from the data of the senses, the second class perceive that the senses are not final, and say, the senses give us representations of things, but what are the things themselves, they cannot tell. The materialist insists on facts, on history, on the force of circumstances, and the animal wants of man; the idealist on the power of Thought and of Will, on inspiration, on miracle, on individual culture. These two modes of thinking are both natural, but the idealist contends that his way of thinking is in higher nature. He concedes all that the other affirms, admits the impressions of sense, admits their coherency, their use and beauty, and then asks the materialist for his grounds of assurance that things are as his senses represent them. But I, he says, affirm facts not affected by the illusions of sense, facts which are of the same nature as the faculty which reports them, and not liable to doubt; facts which in their first appearance to us assume a native superiority to material facts, degrading these into a language by which the first are to be spoken; facts which it only needs a retirement from the senses to discern. Every materialist will be an idealist; but an idealist can never go backward to be a materialist.

The idealist, in speaking of events, sees them as spirits. He does not deny the sensuous fact: by no means; but he will not see that alone. He does not deny the presence of this table, this chair, and the walls of this room, but he looks at these things as the reverse side of the tapestry, as the other end, each being a sequel or completion of a spiritual fact which nearly concerns him. . . .

The materialist, secure in the certainty of sensation, mocks at fine-spun theories, at star-gazers and dreamers, and believes that his life is solid, that he at least takes nothing for granted, but knows where he stands, and what he does. Yet how easy it is to show him, that he also is a phantom walking and working amid phantoms, and that he need only ask a question or two beyond his daily questions, to find his solid universe growing dim and impalpable before his sense. The sturdy capitalist, no matter how deep and square on blocks of Quincy granite he lays the foundations of his banking-house or Exchange, must set it, at last, not on a cube corresponding to the angles of his structure, but on a mass of unknown materials and solidity, red-hot or white-hot, perhaps at the core, which rounds off to an almost perfect sphericity, and lies floating in soft air, and goes spinning away, dragging bank and banker with it at a rate of thousands of miles the hour, he knows not whither,—a bit of bullet, now glimmering, now darkling through a small cubic space on the edge of an unimaginable pit of emptiness. And this wild balloon, in which his whole venture is embarked, is a just symbol of his whole state and faculty. One thing, at least, he says is certain, and does not give me the headache, that figures do not lie; the multiplication table has been hitherto found unimpeachable truth; and, moreover, if I put a gold eagle in my safe, I find it again to-morrow;—but for these thoughts, I know not whence they are. They change and pass away. But ask him why he believes that an uniform experience will continue uniform, or on what grounds he founds his faith in his figures, and he will perceive that his mental fabric is built up on just as strange and quaking foundations as his proud edifice of stone.

In the order of thought, the materialist takes his departure from the external world, and esteems a man as one product of that. The idealist takes his departure from his consciousness, and reckons the world an appearance. The materialist respects sensible masses, Society, Government, social art, and luxury, every establishment, every mass, whether majority of numbers, or extent of space, or amount of objects, every social action. The idealist has another measure, which is metaphysical, namely, the rank which things themselves take in his consciousness; not at all, the size or appearance. Mind is the only reality, of which men and all other natures are better or worse reflectors. Nature, literature, history, are only subjective phenomena. Although in his action overpowered by the laws of action, and so, warmly cooperating with men, even preferring them to himself, yet when he speaks scientifically, or after the order of thought, he is constrained to degrade persons into representatives of truths. He does not respect labor, or the products of labor, namely, property, otherwise than as a manifold symbol, illustrating with wonderful fidelity of details the laws of being; he does not respect government, except as far as it reiterates the law of his mind; nor the church; nor charities; nor arts, for themselves; but hears, as at a vast distance, what they say, as if his consciousness would speak to him through a pantomimic scene. His thought,—that is the Universe. His experience inclines him to behold the procession of facts you call the world, as flowing perpetually outward from an invisible, unsounded center in himself, centre alike of him and of them, and necessitating him to regard all things as having a subjective or relative existence, relative to that aforesaid Unknown Centre of him.

From this transfer of the world into the consciousness, this beholding of all things in the mind, follow easily his whole ethics. It is simpler to be self-dependent. The height, the deity of man is, to be self-sustained, to need no gift, no foreign force. Society is good when it does not violate me; but best when it is likest to solitude. Everything real is self-existent. Everything divine shares the self-existence of Deity. All that you call the world is the shadow of that substance which you are, the perpetual creation of the powers of thought, of those that are dependent and of those that are independent of your will. Do not cumber yourself with fruitless pains to mend and remedy remote effects; let the soul be erect, and all things will go well. You think me the child of my circumstances: I make my circumstance. Let any thought or motive of mine be different from that they are, the difference will transform my condition and economy. I—this thought which is called I,—is the mould into which the world is poured like melted wax. The mould is invisible, but the world betrays the shape of the mould. You call it the power of circumstance, but it is the power of me. Am I in harmony with myself? my position will seem to you just and commanding. Am I vicious and insane? my fortunes will seem to you obscure and descending. As I am, so shall I associate, and, so shall I act; Caesar's history will paint out Caesar. Jesus acted so, because he thought so. I do not wish to overlook or to gainsay any reality; I say, I make my circumstance: but if you ask me, Whence am I? I feel like other men my relation to that Fact which cannot be spoken, or defined, nor even thought, but which exists, and will exist.

The Transcendentalist adopts the whole connection of spiritual doctrine. He believes in miracle, in the perpetual openness of the human mind to new influx of light and power; he believes in inspiration, and in ecstasy.

SHORT WRITINGS ABOUT CHRISTIANITY

In the wake of the birth of Transcendentalism lies traditional and doctrinal Christianity. Here, from various sources, are RWE's estimations of what Christianity had come to mean, was destined to mean, or already meant in his day.

[I]s not Jesus called in Scripture the Mediator? He is the mediator in that only sense in which possibly any being can mediate between God and man,—that is, an instructor of man. He teaches us how to become like God. And a true disciple of Jesus will receive the light he gives most thankfully; but the thanks he offers, and which an exalted being will accept, are not compliments, commemorations, but the use of that instruction. (*from "The Lord's Supper Sermon, September 9, 1832,"* Miscellanies)

* * *

We can never see Christianity from the catechism:—from the pastures, from a boat in the pond, from amidst the songs of wood-birds, we possibly may. Cleansed by the elemental light and wind, steeped in the sea of beautiful forms which the field offers us, we may chance to cast a right glance back upon biography. Christianity is rightly dear to the best of mankind; yet was there never a young philosopher whose breeding had fallen into the Christian church, by whom that brave text of Paul's was not specially prized:—"Then shall also the Son be subject unto Him who put all things under him, that God may be all in all." Let the claims and virtues of persons be never so great and welcome, the instinct of man presses eagerly onward to the impersonal and illimitable, and gladly arms itself against the dogmatism of bigots with this generous word out of the book itself. (*from "Circles,"* Essays: First)

* * *

For the Universe has three children, born at one time, which reappear, under different names, in every system of thought, whether they be called cause, operation, and effect; or, more poetically, Jove, Pluto, Neptune; or, theologically, the Father, the Spirit, and the Son; but which we will call here, the Knower, the Doer, and the Sayer. These stand respectively for the love of truth, for the love of good, and for the love of beauty. These three are equal. Each is that which he is essentially, so that he cannot be surmounted or analyzed, and each of these three has the power of the others latent in him, and his own patent. (*from "The Poet,"* Essays: Second)

* * *

This selection is not only about what RWE believed about mid-nineteenth century Christianity, but how to judge whether a teaching of Jesus in the gospels was intended to become a lasting rite or sacrament.

Whilst I am upon this topic, I cannot help remarking that it is not a little singular that we should have preserved this rite and insisted upon perpetuating one symbolical act of Christ whilst we have totally neglected all others—particularly one other which had at least an equal claim to our observance. Jesus washed the feet of his disciples and told them that, as he had washed their feet, they ought to wash one another's feet; for he had given them an example, that they should do as he had done to them. I ask any person who believes the Supper to have been designed by Jesus to be commemorated forever, to go and read the account of it in the other Gospels, and then compare with it the account of this transaction in St. John, and tell me if this be not much more explicitly authorized than the Supper. It only differs in this, that we have found the Supper used in New England and the washing of the feet not. But if we had found it an established rite in our churches, on grounds of mere authority, it would have been impossible to have argued against it. That rite is used by the Church of Rome, and by the Sandemanians. It has been very properly dropped by other Christians. Why? For two reasons: (1) because it was a local custom, and unsuitable in western countries; and (2) because it was typical, and all understand that humility is the thing signified. But the Passover was local too, and does not concern us, and its bread and wine were typical, and do not help us to understand the redemption which they signified. *(from "The Lord's Supper Sermon, September 9, 1832,"* Miscellanies)

* * *

Theodore Parker "was a more important influence than any other Transcendentalist on the so-called Social Gospel movement within liberal Protestantism toward the end of the nineteenth century."[42] *This is taken from RWE's funeral oration, published as "Theodore Parker," in* Miscellanies.

His commanding merit as a reformer is this, that he insisted beyond all men in pulpits,—I cannot think of one rival,—that the essence of Christianity is its practical morals; it is there for use, or it is nothing; and if you combine it with sharp trading, or with ordinary city ambitions to gloze over municipal corruptions, or private intemperance, or successful fraud, or immoral politics, or unjust wars, or the cheating of Indians, or the robbery of frontier nations, or leaving your principles at home to follow on the high seas or in Europe a supple complaisance to tyrants,—it is a hypocrisy, and the truth is not in you; and no love of religious music or of dreams of Swedenborg, or praise of John Wesley, or of Jeremy Taylor, can save you from the Satan which you are.

* * *

The importance ascribed to this particular ordinance [Communion] is not consistent with the spirit of Christianity. The general object and effect of the ordinance is unexceptionable. It has

been, and is, I doubt not, the occasion of indefinite good; but an
importance is given by Christians to it which never can belong to
any form. My friends, the apostle well assures us that "the kingdom of God is not meat and drink, but righteousness and peace
and joy in the Holy Ghost." I am not so foolish as to declaim
against forms. Forms are as essential as bodies; but to exalt particular forms, to adhere to one form a moment after it is outgrown, is unreasonable, and it is alien to the spirit of Christ. If I
understand the distinction of Christianity, the reason why it is to
be preferred over all other systems and is divine is this, that it is
a moral system; that it presents men with truths which are their
own reason, and enjoins practices that are their own justifica-
tion; that if miracles may be said to have been its evidence to the
first Christians, they are not its evidence to us, but the doctrines
themselves; that every practice is Christian which praises itself,
and every practice unchristian which condemns itself. I am not
engaged to Christianity by decent forms, or saving ordinances;
it is not usage, it is not what I do not understand, that binds me
to it,—let these be the sandy foundations of falsehoods. What I
revere and obey in it is its reality, its boundless charity, its deep
interior life, the rest it gives to mind, the echo it returns to my
thoughts, the perfect accord it makes with my reason through all
its representation of God and His Providence; and the persua-
sion and courage that come out thence to lead me upward and
onward. Freedom is the essence of this faith. It has for its object
simply to make men good and wise. Its institutions then should
be as flexible as the wants of men. That form out of which the
life and suitableness have departed, should be as worthless in its
eyes as the dead leaves that are falling around us. (*from "The
Lord's Supper Sermon, September 9, 1832,"* Miscellanies)

* * *

*These paragraphs and sentences are taken from a lon-
ger critique of the Anglican Church, the national church, of*

England—but RWE's comments sound prophetically similar to those of Christendom's critics in our own day.

In seeing old castles and cathedrals, I sometimes say, as today, in front of Dundee Church tower, which is eight hundred years old, "this was built by another and a better race than any that now look on it." And, plainly, there has been great power of sentiment at work in this island, of which these buildings are the proofs: as volcanic basalts show the work of fire which has been extinguished for ages. England felt the full heat of the Christianity which fermented Europe, and drew, like the chemistry of fire, a firm line between barbarism and culture. The power of the religious sentiment put an end to human sacrifices, checked appetite, inspired the crusades, inspired resistance to tyrants, inspired self-respect, set bounds to serfdom and slavery, founded liberty, created the religious architecture,—York, Newstead, Westminster, Fountains Abbey, Ripon, Beverley, and Dundee,—works to which the key is lost, with the sentiment which created them; inspired the English Bible, the liturgy, the monkish histories, the chronicle of Richard of Devizes. The priest translated the Vulgate, and translated the sanctities of old hagiology into English virtues on English ground. It was a certain affirmative or aggressive state of the Caucasian races. Man awoke refreshed by the sleep of ages. . . .

Good churches are not built by bad men; at least, there must be probity and enthusiasm somewhere in the society. These minsters were neither built nor filled by atheists. No church has had more learned, industrious or devoted men; plenty of "clerks and bishops, who, out of their gowns, would turn their backs on no man." Their architecture still glows with faith in immortality. Heats and genial periods arrive in history, or, shall we say, plentitudes of Divine Presence, by which high tides are caused in the human spirit, and great virtues and talents appear, as in the eleventh, twelfth, thirteenth, and again in the sixteenth and seventeenth centuries, when the nation was full of genius and piety.

But the age of the Wicliffes, Cobhams, Arundels, Beckets; of the Latimers, Mores, Cranmers; of the Taylors, Leightons, Herberts; of the Sherlocks, and Butlers, is gone. Silent revolutions in opinion have made it impossible that men like these should return, or find a place in their once sacred stalls. The spirit that dwelt in this church has glided away to animate other activities; and they who come to the old shrines find apes and players rustling the old garments. . . .

The church at this moment is much to be pitied. She has nothing left but possession. (*from "Religion,"* Traits)

"BLOWS AGAINST FALSE THEOLOGY" (ADMIRATION FOR ROBERT BURNS)

Perhaps because he was a Scot himself, RWE showed more admiration for Robert Burns than for the English poets then writing who were more popular in America. More likely, however, were the reasons he articulates here, demonstrating how Burns represents a spiritual connection to the freedom of humankind when it is able to truly meet the wild Spirit of God. A final note: Reading these paragraphs might make any person desire a eulogizer like RWE! From "Robert Burns," in Miscellanies.

Robert Burns, the poet of the middle class, re-presents in the mind of men to-day that great uprising of the middle class against the armed and privileged minorities, that uprising which worked politically in the American and French Revolutions, and which, not in governments so much as in education and social order, has changed the face of the world.

In order for this destiny, his birth, breeding and fortunes were low. His organic sentiment was absolute independence, and resting as it should on a life of labor. No man existed who could look down on him. They that looked into his eyes saw that they might look down the sky as easily. His muse and teaching was common sense, joyful, aggressive, irresistible. Not Latimer, nor

Luther struck more telling blows against false theology than did this brave singer. The Confession of Augsburg, the Declaration of Independence, the French Rights of Man, and the Marseillaise, are not more weighty documents in the history of freedom than the songs of Burns. His satire has lost none of its edge. His musical arrows yet sing through the air. He is so substantially a reformer that I find his grand plain sense in close chain with the greatest masters,—Rabelais, Shakespeare in comedy, Cervantes, Butler, and Burns. If I should add another name, I find it only in a living countryman of Burns.

He is an exceptional genius. The people who care nothing for literature and poetry care for Burns. It was indifferent—they thought who saw him—whether he wrote verse or not: he could have done anything else as well. Yet how true a poet is he! And the poet, too, of poor men, of gray hodden and the guernsey coat and the blouse. He has given voice to all the experiences of common life; he has endeared the farmhouse and cottage, patches and poverty, beans and barley; ale, the poor man's wine; hardship; the fear of debt; the dear society of weans and wife, of brothers and sisters, proud of each other, knowing so few and finding amends for want and obscurity in books and thoughts. What a love of Nature, and, shall I say it? of middle-class Nature. Not like Goethe, in the stars, or like Byron, in the ocean, or Moore, in the luxurious East, but in the homely landscape which the poor see around them,—bleak leagues of pasture and stubble, ice and sleet and rain and snow-choked brooks; birds, hares, field-mice, thistles and heather, which he daily knew. How many "Bonny Doons" and "John Anderson my jo's" and "Auld lang synes" all around the earth have his verses been applied to! And his love-songs still woo and melt the youths and maids; the farm-work, the country holiday, the fishing-cobble are still his debtors today.

And as he was thus the poet of the poor, anxious, cheerful, working humanity, so had he the language of low life. He grew up in a rural district, speaking a patois unintelligible to all but natives, and he has made the Lowland Scotch a Doric dialect of fame. It is the only example in history of a language made classic by the genius of a single man. But more than this. He had that secret of genius to draw from the bottom of society the strength of its speech, and astonish the ears of the polite with these artless words, better than art, and filtered of all offence through his beauty. It seemed odious to Luther that the devil should have all the best tunes; he would bring them into the churches; and Burns knew how to take from fairs and gypsies, black-smiths and drovers, the speech of the market and street, and clothe it with melody. But I am detaining you too long. The memory of Burns,—I am afraid heaven and earth have taken too good care of it to leave us anything to say. The west winds are murmuring it. Open the windows behind you, and hearken for the incoming tide, what the waves say of it. The doves perching always on the eaves of the Stone Chapel opposite, may know something about it. Every name in broad Scotland keeps his fame bright. The memory of Burns,—every man's, every boy's and girl's head carries snatches of his songs, and they say them by heart, and, what is strangest of all, never learned them from a book, but from mouth to mouth. The wind whispers them, the birds whistle them, the corn, barley, and bulrushes hoarsely rustle them, nay, the music-boxes at Geneva are framed and toothed to play them; the hand-organs of the Savoyards in all cities repeat them, and the chimes of hells ring them in the spires. They are the property and the solace of mankind.

6

Memorable Aphorisms

One would rather be "A pagan, suckled in a creed outworn," than to be defrauded of his manly right in coming into nature. (from "Divinity School Address," *Nature*)

In all my lectures, I have taught one doctrine, namely, the infinitude of the private man. (from private journals; see note 29)

Life only avails, not the having lived. Power ceases in the instant of repose; it resides in the moment of transition from a past to a new state, in the shooting of a gulf, in the darting to an aim. This one fact the world hates, that the soul *becomes*. (from "Self-Reliance," *Essays: First*)

Nothing can bring you peace but yourself. Nothing can bring you peace but the triumph of principles. (from "Self-Reliance," *Essays: First*)

Why should we not also enjoy an original relation to the universe? Why should we not have a poetry and philosophy of insight and not of tradition, and a religion by revelation to us, and not the history of theirs? (from "Nature," *Nature*)

We must go alone. I like the silent church before the service begins, better than any preaching. (from "Self-Reliance," *Essays: First*)

The aspect of Nature is devout. Like the figure of Jesus, she stands with bended head, and hands folded upon the breast. The happiest man is he who learns from nature the lesson of worship. (from "Spirit," *Nature*)

We distinguish the announcements of the soul, its manifestations of its own nature, by the term "Revelation." These are always attended by the emotion of the sublime. For this communication is an influx of the Divine mind into our mind. (from "The Over-Soul," *Essays: First*)

Of immortality, the soul, when well employed, is incurious. It is so well, that it is sure it will be well. It asks no questions of the Supreme Power. (from "Worship," *Conduct*)

Man is a stream whose source is hidden. Our being is descending into us from we know not whence. (from "The Over-Soul," *Essays: First*)

Ineffable is the union of man and God in every act of the soul. The simplest person, who in his integrity worships God, becomes God; yet for ever and ever the influx of this better and universal self is new and unsearchable. (from "The Over-Soul," *Essays: First*)

We learn that God IS; that he is in me; and that all things are shadows of him. (from "Circles," *Essays: First*)

Life is a series of surprises, and would not be worth taking or keeping, if it were not. God delights to isolate us every day, and hide from us the past and the future. (from "Experience," *Essays: Second*)

Though we travel the world over to find the beautiful, we must carry it with us, or we find it not. (from "Art," *Essays: First*)

Saints are sad, because they behold sin, (even when they speculate,) from the point of view of the conscience, and not of the intellect. . . . The conscience must feel it as essence, essential evil. This it is not: it has an objective existence, but no subjective. (from "Experience," *Essays: Second*)

Belief consists in accepting the affirmations of the soul; unbelief, in denying them. (from "Montaigne; or, the Skeptic," *Representative Men*)

In the progress of the character, there is an increasing faith in the moral sentiment, and a decreasing faith in propositions. (from "Worship," *Conduct*)

[T]he essence of Christianity is its practical morals; it is there for use, or it is nothing. (from "Theodore Parker," *Miscellanies*)

In the woods, we return to reason and faith. (from "Nature," *Nature*)

"At the gates of the forest, the surprised man of the world is forced to leave his city estimates of great and small, wise and foolish. The knapsack of custom falls off his back with the first step he takes into these precincts. Here is sanctity which shames our religions, and reality which discredits our heroes." (from "Nature," *Nature*)

I unsettle all things. No facts are to me sacred; none are profane; I simply experiment, an endless seeker, with no Past at my back. (from "Circles," *Essays: First*)

Standing on the bare ground,—my head bathed by the blithe air, and uplifted into infinite space,—all mean egotism vanishes. I become a transparent eyeball; I am nothing; I see all; the currents of the Universal Being circulate through me; I am part or particle of God. (from "Nature," *Nature*)

That is always best which gives me to myself. The sublime is excited in me by the great stoical doctrine, Obey thyself. (from "Divinity School Address," *Nature*)

Notes

1. Robert D. Richardson, Jr. *Emerson: The Mind on Fire* (Berkeley: University of California Press, 1995), 8–9.

2. Joel Myerson, ed., *The Selected Letters of Ralph Waldo Emerson* (New York: Columbia University Press, 1997), 114.

3. This point is made most effectively by T. S. McMillin, *Our Preposterous Use of Literature: Emerson and the Nature of Reading* (Urbana: University of Illinois Press, 2000), 76.

4. See the excellent new Tim Flinders, ed., *Henry David Thoreau: Spiritual and Prophetic Writings* (Maryknoll, NY: Orbis Books, 2015), in which Chapter 1 is devoted to excerpts from Thoreau's journals and letters.

5. Richardson, *Emerson*, 110.

6. Weslery T. Mott, ed., *The Complete Sermons of Ralph Waldo Emerson, Vol. 4* (Columbia: University of Missouri Press, 1992), 192.

7. Lawrence Buell, *Emerson* (Cambridge, MA: Harvard University Press, 2003), 16.

8. Emerson was deeply impacted, as were Thoreau and Whitman a decade or two after him, by the British writer and amateur Sanskrit scholar, Charles Wilkins's translation of the Gita, first published in London in 1785. See Richard H. Davis, *The Bhagavad Gita: A Biography* (Princeton, NJ: Princeton University Press, 2014), 74–76.

9. William James, "Address at the Centenary of RWE," in *Writings 1902–1910* (New York: Library of America, 1987), 1122.

10. Jay Tolson, *Pilgrim in the Ruins: A Life of Walker Percy* (New York: Simon and Schuster, 1992), 466.

11. See Lawrence Buell, ed., *The American Transcendentalists: Essential Writings* (New York: Modern Library, 2006), xxii.

12. From "Journal B"; see Ralph Waldo Emerson, *Selected Journals 1820–1842* (New York, Penguin Group), 483.

13. Robert Lowell, "Concord," first published in *Partisan Review* X (1943), 316. See Frank Bidart and David Gewanter, eds., *Robert*

Lowell: Collected Poems, (New York: Farrar, Straus and Giroux, 2003), 1152.

14. James, "Address at the Centenary of RWE," 1119.

15. Henry Versluis, *American Gurus: From Transcendentalism to New Age Religion* (New York: Oxford University Press, 2014), 2.

16. See Anthony Domestico, "Blessings in Disguise: The Unfashionable Genius of Marilynne Robinson," *Commonweal*, November 14, 2014, 12.

17. Quoted in Sydney E. Ahlstrom and Jonathan S. Carey, *An American Reformation: A Documentary History of Unitarian Christianity* (Middletown, CT: Wesleyan University Press, 1985), 5.

18. Whitman and Poe, in David LaRocca, ed., *Estimating Emerson* (New York, Bloomsbury Academic, 2013), 176 and 45. Poe also wrote a short story in 1841 lampooning the earnestness of early Transcendentalists, "Never Bet the Devil Your Head," poking fun at the notion that stories were always supposed to be communicating spiritual truths.

19. John Dewey, in LaRocca, *Estimating Emerson,* 296.

20. George Santayana, in ibid.; 298, 299, 301.

21. Friedrich Nietzsche, in ibid.; 283, 273. The second quotation is from Nietzsche's private notebooks.

22. John Dewey, in ibid., 295.

23. Henry James, *Hawthorne* (New York: Macmillan, 1909), 31.

24. See Michelle Latiolais's Introduction, *Butcher's Crossing* (New York: New York Review Books, 2007), xv. It is also interesting how Will observes, early in the novel, that his reading of the Bible happened, not because his father encouraged him to do so during childhood, but by inspiration from Emerson. Ibid., 45.

25. James, "Address at the Centenary of RWE," 1124.

26. Buell, *Emerson*, 36.

27. Ronald A. Bosco, ed.,*The Complete Sermons of Ralph Waldo Emerson, Vol. 3* (Columbia: University of Missouri Press, 1991), sermon cxxxv, 268.

28. Buell, *Emerson*, 5.

29. From "Journal E"; see Emerson, *Selected Journals 1820–1842*, 735–36.

30. Buel, *The American Transcendentalists*; xii.

31. Robert D. Richardson, *William James: In the Maelstrom of American Modernism* (Boston: Houghton Mifflin, 2006), 157.

32. Robert Frost, in LaRocca, *Estimating Emerson*, 459.

33. E. Vernon Arnold, *Roman Stoicism* (New York: Cambridge University Press, 1911), 330, 332.

34. James, "Address at the Centenary of RWE," 1122.

35. Plutarch, "Consolation to His Wife," in James Loeb et al., eds., *Moralia* (Cambridge, MA: Harvard University Press, 1959), 575–605.

36. Lyndall Gordon, *T. S. Eliot: An Imperfect Life* (New York: W. W. Norton, 2000), 340.

37. From "Journal E"; see Emerson, *Selected Journals 1820–1842*, 767.

38. Mary Oliver, in La Rocca, *Estimating Emerson*, 13. On Emerson and Goethe, see Richardson, *Emerson*, 221–23.

39. From the section of "Manuscript Poems 1840–1849," in Ralph Waldo Emerson, *Collected Poems and Translations* (New York: Library of America, 1994), 366.

40. From "Journal E"; see Emerson, *Selected Journals 1820–1842*, 767.

41. These are references to terms used by Thomas Aquinas in the *Summa Theologica*. See Volume 9, Angels: 1a. 50–64.

42. Buell, *The American Transcendentalists*, xvii.

MODERN SPIRITUAL MASTERS
Robert Ellsberg, Series Editor

This series introduces the essential writing and vision of some of the great spiritual teachers of our time. While many of these figures are rooted in long-established traditions of spirituality, others have charted new, untested paths. In each case, however, they have engaged in a spiritual journey shaped by the challenges and concerns of our age. Together with the saints and witnesses of previous centuries, these modern spiritual masters may serve as guides and companions to a new generation of seekers.

Already published:

Thich Nhat Hanh (edited by Robert Ellsberg)
Abraham Joshua Heschel (edited by Susannah Heschel)
Etty Hillesum (edited by Annemarie S. Kidder)
Caryll Houselander (edited by Wendy M. Wright)
Pope John XXIII (edited by Jean Maalouf)
Rufus Jones (edited by Kerry Walters)
Clarence Jordan (edited by Joyce Hollyday)
John Main (edited by Laurence Freeman)
Anthony de Mello (edited by William Dych, S.J.)
Thomas Merton (edited by Christine M. Bochen)
John Muir (edited by Tim Flinders)
John Henry Newman (edited by John T. Ford, C.S.C.)
Henri Nouwen (edited by Robert A. Jonas)
Flannery O'Connor (edited by Robert Ellsberg)
Karl Rahner (edited by Philip Endean)
Brother Roger of Taizé (edited by Marcello Fidanzio)
Oscar Romero (by Marie Dennis, Rennie Golden, and Scott Wright)
Albert Schweitzer (edited by James Brabazon)
Frank Sheed and Maisie Ward (edited by David Meconi)
Sadhu Sundar Singh (edited by Charles E. Moore)
Mother Maria Skobtsova (introduction by Jim Forest)
Dorothee Soelle (edited by Dianne L. Oliver)
Edith Stein (edited by John Sullivan, O.C.D.)
David Steindl-Rast (edited by Clare Hallward)
William Stringfellow (edited by Bill Wylie-Kellerman)
Pierre Teilhard de Chardin (edited by Ursula King)
Mother Teresa (edited by Jean Maalouf)
St. Thérèse of Lisieux (edited by Mary Frohlich)
Phyllis Tickle (edited by Jon M. Sweeney)
Henry David Thoreau (edited by Tim Flinders)
Howard Thurman (edited by Mary Krohlich)
Leo Tolstoy (edited by Charles E. Moore)
Evelyn Underhill (edited by Emilie Griffin)
Vincent Van Gogh (by Carol Berry)
Jean Vanier (edited by Carolyn Whitney-Brown)
Swami Vivekananda (edited by Victor M. Parachin)
Simone Weil (edited by Eric O. Springsted)
John Howard Yoder (edited by Paul Martens and Jenny Howells)